RULERS OF THE MIDDLE AGES

WILLIAM THE CONQUEROR

Last Invader of England

Tom McGowen

Enslow Publishers, Inc.
40 Industrial Road
Box 398
Berkeley Heights, NJ 07922
USA

http://www.enslow.com

To the staff at the Eisenhower Public Library in Norridge, Illinois

Library of Congress Cataloging-in-Publication Data:

McGowen, Tom.
    William the Conqueror : last invader of England / Tom McGowen.
        p. cm. — (Rulers of the Middle Ages)
    Includes bibliographical references and index.
    ISBN-13: 978-0-7660-2713-8
    ISBN-10: 0-7660-2713-9
    1. William I, King of England, 1027 or 8–1087—Juvenile literature. 2. Great Britain—
Kings and rulers—Biography—Juvenile literature. 3. Great Britain—History—William I,
1066–1087—Juvenile literature. I. Title. II. Series.
DA197.M44 2006
942.02'1092—dc22
[B]

                                                        2006014965

Printed in the United States of America

10 9 8 7 6 5 4 3 2 1

To Our Readers:
We have done our best to make sure all Internet addresses in this book were active and appropriate
when we went to press. However, the author and the publisher have no control over and assume
no liability for the material available on those Internet sites or on other Web sites they may link
to. Any comments or suggestions can be sent by e-mail to comments@enslow.com or to the
address on the back cover.

Illustration Credits: Clipart.com, pp. 7, 115; Enslow Publishers, Inc., pp. 14, 111; Original
Painting by Corey R. Wolfe, p. 4; iStockphoto.com, p. 29; © JupiterImages, Inc., p. 127; © Mary
Evans Picture Library/The Image Works, pp. 35, 45, 103, 107; © Museum of London/Topham-
HIP/The Image Works, pp. 125, 137; Selected by Jim Harter, *Nautical Illustrations,* published by
Dover Publications, Inc., in 2003, p. 82; Wikipedia Commons, pp. 12, 19, 70, 72, 83, 95.

Illustration Used in Design: Reproduced from *Full-Color Picture Sourcebook of Historic
Ornament,* published by Dover Publications, Inc.

Cover Illustration: Original painting by Corey R. Wolfe.

CONTENTS

William came from a long line of warriors and would grow into a great conqueror himself.

A Conqueror Is Born

SOME ELEVEN HUNDRED YEARS AGO, ON A DARK, moonless night, a cluster of ships came gliding out of the sea toward the coast of France. They looked like swimming dragons, long and sleek, with carved grinning dragon heads on slender necks at their fronts. Each ship carried about eighty men—hard-faced men, dressed in furs and leather, with swords, spears, and axes in their fists and metal helmets on their heads.

For four hundred years, from the late 700s to about the beginning of the 1100s, the people of much of Europe lived every day—and especially the nights—in cowering fear of attacks by ships such as these. The men in these ships were sea raiders. They made sudden surprise attacks on towns and cities, going on a rampage of robbery, murder, and destruction. These attackers came from what are now the northern nations of Denmark, Norway, and Sweden, and were known as Northmen, or Norsemen.

The Norsemen were superbly skillful sailors and builders of sleek, swift boats. In fleets of ten or more ships, they sailed up rivers, generally at night, until they reached a town or city. Then, leaping from the ships, they attacked, with swords and axes swinging. Most men who tried to stop them were mercilessly cut down. They broke into churches and homes of nobles and wealthy citizens as well as homes of ordinary people, and looted them of anything of value. Generally, they set the building afire when they left. Women and children were often taken prisoner and carried off to become slaves. At times the Norse warriors inflicted a horrible form of death by torture that they called the "blood eagle." This consisted of chopping a man's ribs loose from his spine and pulling his lungs out and spreading them on his back like bloody wings.[1]

NORSEMEN INVADE FRANCE

Attacks by the Norsemen left communities in shock; they were robbed and looted, with burning buildings and streets littered with corpses. Throughout most of Europe, at every church service for several hundred years, a special prayer was always spoken by the priests—"God, spare us from the fury of the Northmen!" A poet, writing in the year 1000, called this time, "A sword age, a wind age, a wolf age. No longer is there mercy among men."[2] These men, who caused so much terror, were the men who became known as Vikings, later in history.

In the early days of the tenth century (the 900s) a force of Norsemen landed in the northern part of France, near

THE BLOODTHIRSTY NORSEMEN

Whereas most of the nations of Western Europe belonged to the Christian Church eleven hundred years ago, the northern lands of Norway, Sweden, and Denmark believed in their own gods, such as Odin All-Father, Thor, and Frey. These were gods who stood for war and battle. According to Norse religion, a man who was killed in a battle was taken to a heaven ruled over by Odin, where he spent the rest of eternity feasting and fighting—for fun!

Thus, Norse warriors were perfectly willing to risk their lives in battle. They wanted to show how brave and fierce they were, so that Odin would reward them. They gloried in bloodshed. Their chieftains had nicknames such as Eric Blood-Axe, Thorfinn Skullsplitter, and Bjorn Ironside. Many Norse warriors gave their swords and axes names such as "Brain-Biter," "Long-and-Sharp," and "War Flame."

Some of these Norse warriors were men known as berserkers, which meant "bear skins." These men were said to wear cloaks made of bear fur, and to fight like enraged bears, giving no thought to danger or injury. It was said that they gnashed their teeth, bit their swords, and shrieked and howled when they went into battle. Their name has come down to us as the English word berserk, which means to be taken over by wild fury or madness.

the city of Rouen, in what was then called the Kingdom of the West Franks. Their leader was named Hrolf or Rolf. Legends that have come down to us about him say that he was so huge, so tall and broad, that no horse could carry his weight, and he had to walk instead of being able to ride. Thus, he was known to his fellow Norsemen by nicknames such as Big Rolf Go-Afoot, or Marching Rolf.

Rolf and his men set up a permanent encampment on the coast of the Frankish Kingdom. From this base they began making raids on nearby villages and even on the city of Rouen. From time to time, more Norsemen would land on the coast and join Rolf, making his force more powerful. In time, the entire region was nearly destroyed by raids. Farms were deserted. Monasteries were abandoned and in ruins, the monks having taken whatever they could carry and fled.

THE FRENCH KING MAKES AN OFFER

Finally, the king of the West Franks, a man known as Charles the Simple, decided he had to do something. He arranged to have a peaceful meeting with Rolf and made him an offer. He offered to give the whole region to the Norsemen and let Rolf rule it. In return, Rolf had to agree to swear allegiance to the king, becoming what was called his vassal, a man who owed Charles loyalty and obedience. Rolf also had to agree to become a Christian. He accepted, and the king officially made him a count, a nobleman ranking about three places below a king. A region ruled by a count was generally called a county.

This turned out to be a very good move for the king, for Rolf, and for the French people of the region. Since the towns and cities Rolf had been raiding now belonged to him, he no longer had to raid them to get the things he and his men needed. He became more interested in helping them become more prosperous. The people of the region no longer had to worry about being killed or having their homes burned by Rolf's men. Rolf's rule actually brought peace and security. However, like most rulers of the time, he ruled sternly. Crimes such as stealing or assaulting people were punished brutally, by having hands cut off or eyes put out.

Technically, the land that Charles the Simple had given Rolf was still part of the Kingdom of the West Franks, but Rolf could do as he wanted in it. He gave areas of the land, often including villages, to many of his favorite warriors. This gave the men wealth and power. Thus, Rolf had created a nobility, or group who ruled over their lands in his name and owed allegiance to him. These nobles had the titles of viscounts, meaning assistant-counts.

THE NORSEMEN CHANGE THEIR WAYS

Because the region Rolf had been given was now occupied and ruled by Norsemen, it soon became known to the people of the rest of France as Normandy, the place of Northmen. The people of Normandy were called Normans. Rolf's men were mostly Danes with a sprinkling of Norwegians, so they all spoke Norse. But there were very few Norse women among them, so they married

9

LAND FOR LOYALTY

The way of life for the people of Western Europe when Rolf became Count of Normandy was what we now call feudalism. It was based on ownership of land. Land was very important because it was the main source for food, building materials, cloth, and everything required for life. Thus, it was the basic source of wealth. Under feudalism, all the land in a region belonged to the ruler of the region, but he could give it out in small amounts to people. In return for the land, the people would become the ruler's vassals, owing him loyalty and allegiance. This included serving as soldiers for him in time of war and providing services for him when needed. Vassals given land could in turn give portions of it to other people who then became their vassals.

French women. They began learning French; and when their children were born, they grew up speaking mostly French with their mothers.

As generations passed, French became the language of Normandy, and most of the descendants of the Norsemen could no longer even speak any Norse. The name of their famous leader, Rolf, was even changed to a French form of it, Rollo. Also, the worship of the Old Norse gods gradually faded away as more and more Normans converted to Christianity. They even began rebuilding many of the monasteries and churches their fathers and grandfathers had destroyed. Rollo's son, known as William Longsword, rebuilt the Abbey of Jumièges near Rouen, which his father had nearly destroyed. It was said that he seriously considered becoming a monk there. The Normans became passionate Christians.

After several generations, the mixture of Norse and French blood actually seemed to have produced a new kind of people, with their own distinctive ways. An Italian writer who lived in the 1000s said of them, "they are passionately fond of hawking, of riding, of warlike armor, and of splendid garments."[3] He accused them of being greedy for riches and land. Another writer said they were "given to hunting and hawking and delighting in horses and accoutrements and fine clothing."[4] He charged that they were "eager for gain and eager for power." An Englishman who lived in the late 1000s, said, "They are a race inured (accustomed) to war, and can hardly live without it, fierce in attacking their enemies."[5] He also remarked that they were "exceedingly particular in their dress." It sounds as if the Normans actually enjoyed warfare, wanted to dominate other people, and loved to be well dressed.

JOINED BY A MARRIAGE

Upon the death of Rollo, in about 931, his oldest son, William Longsword, became count. From then on, the oldest living son of the man who was count was always regarded as the heir and would become the next count when his father died. However, by the beginning of the 1000s, the great-grandson of Rollo was ruling Normandy and calling himself duke, a noble rank higher than a count

IN·SINV·TEMPLI·ROLLO·QVIESCIT
A·SE VASTATAE·CONDITAE NORMANNIAE·PATER·AC·PRIMVS DVX
LABORI QVI·FRACTVS·OCCVBVIT·OCTOGENARIO MAIOR·AN·CM XXIII

Today, people may view Rollo's coffin in Normandy, France.

and just below a prince. The other male members of the family all had the title of count. With Normandy now ruled by a duke, it became the kind of territory called a dukedom, or duchy.

In 1002, the sister of a Norman duke became the queen of England. England lies straight across from Normandy and France on the other side of the strip of sea called the English Channel. The people of England at the beginning of the 1000s were known as Anglo-Saxons. They were the descendants of three tribes of people—the Angles, Saxons, and Jutes—who came from what are now regions of Germany and invaded and conquered England in the 500s. They spoke a German-sounding language we now call Old

English. England gets its name from two Old English words, *Engla lond*, that meant "land of the Angles." In 1000, most of England was a kingdom, ruled by a king named Ethelred. In 1002, Ethelred married Emma, the sister of Duke Richard II of Normandy, and made her his queen.

Some seven years later, a king of Denmark called Sweyn Forkbeard led a great invasion into England. England had been a target for Danish invasions for several hundred years. It lay directly in line with Denmark, and all Danes had to do was launch their ships and sail straight west across the North Sea to reach it. There were many Danes living in the northeastern part of England, descended from Danes who had invaded in the 800s and 900s. Most of them hailed Sweyn as England's new king and swarmed to join his army. As this Danish army tramped through England, most English people simply gave up and also hailed Sweyn as king.

A BABY BOY IS BORN

By 1013, England was almost completely conquered. By that time, Ethelred and Emma had three children, two boys named Edward and Alfred, and a girl named Goda. Ethelred sent Emma and the children to live in Normandy with her brother Duke Richard, to keep them all safe. Ethelred stayed in England to try to fight to keep his throne. His eldest son, Edmund, by an earlier wife, stayed with him.

Ethelred died in 1016, Edmund died shortly later, and England was ruled by Danish kings for the next twenty-six

years. The Dane who became king of England when
Ethelred died was a man named Cnut, or Canute, the son
of Sweyn Forkbeard. Shortly after becoming king, Cnut
did something that is now hard to understand. He did not
know Ethelred's former wife Emma—the mother of
Edward, Alfred, and Goda—and had never even seen her.
Yet, he invited her to come to England and marry him,

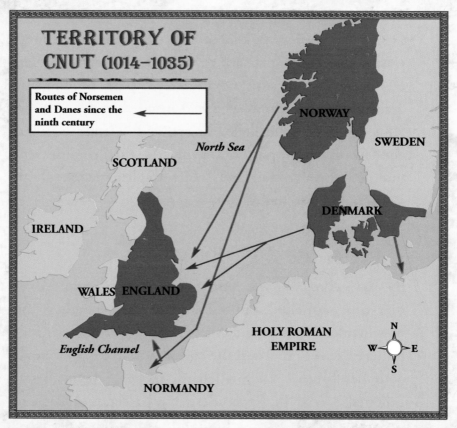

TERRITORY OF
CNUT (1014–1035)

Routes of Norsemen
and Danes since the
ninth century

NORWAY

SWEDEN

North Sea

SCOTLAND

DENMARK

IRELAND

WALES ENGLAND

HOLY ROMAN
EMPIRE

English Channel

N
W   E
S

NORMANDY

By 1035, the Norsemen and Danes had conquered much of
England from their homelands of Norway and Denmark.
They also had raided Normandy and parts of the Holy Roman
Empire, which included present-day Germany.

making her queen again! Some historians have believed Cnut did this to try to make the English people more loyal to him. Others think he may have been trying for an alliance with Normandy. Whatever the reason, Emma accepted his proposal and they were married in 1017. Her three children continued to live in Normandy for many more years.

Duke Richard died in 1026, and his eldest son became Duke Richard III. However, he died a year later, and his younger brother, Robert, became duke. The exact date is not known, but in 1027 or 1028, Robert became the father of a baby boy. The boy was apparently christened with the French name Guillaume, but at that time, throughout most of Europe, most writing was in Latin, and Guillaume was written as Willelmus. It has come down to us in English as William. This baby would grow up to become the man known as William the Conqueror.

GROWING UP IN DANGER

WILLIAM WAS ROBERT'S FIRSTBORN SON, SO AS long as he was alive he would always be the eldest son. But even though William was Robert's oldest son, no one expected him to ever become duke. His mother was a commoner, a girl named Arlette, or Herleve, who was the daughter of a leather-maker, and was not even married to Duke Robert. This seemed to eliminate William from ever being duke. He was not considered to be Robert's official son, so he could not be Robert's heir to become duke.

It was common in those days for kings, dukes, and other people of importance, to be given nicknames that described something about them. The nickname of the French king who had given Normandy to the Norse chieftain, Rollo, had been Charles the Simple, because he seemed a bit foolish. The nickname of William's father, Duke Robert, was "Robert the Magnificent." This was because Robert was the sort of person who did everything with great style. He dressed in rich and colorful clothing, deliberately did things that called attention to himself, and often did things that were a total surprise to everyone. He provided a surprise when he was about twenty-five years old and William was just seven. Calling together all the counts and viscounts who ruled parts of Normandy under him, he made an announcement. He told them that he intended to make a pilgrimage, or religious journey, to what Christians called the Holy City, Jerusalem, in what is the present-day nation of Israel.

THE DANGERS OF A PILGRIMAGE

Many Christians made religious pilgrimages at that time. It was believed to be a way of helping them get into heaven after they died. However, most pilgrimages were made to holy places and the tombs of saints in Europe, which were fairly easy to reach.

A pilgrimage to the Holy Land was a long, dangerous journey, not usually made by people in very important positions, such as kings and dukes. It took people through countries where there were bandits and thieves, and into climates where diseases that Westerners could not easily fight off were common. Many of those who went to the Holy Land never returned. Only twenty-seven years before, the count of the French province of Brittany had gone on a pilgrimage from which he did not return. Robert's followers begged him not to go. They were afraid something might happen to him, and Normandy would be left without a duke, for there was no heir who could become duke. Robert had no brother, and no son other than William. His closest relatives were cousins, and this could become a situation that could cause civil war, with cousins fighting each other to become the duke.

Robert assured his followers that he had a plan to make sure Normandy would have a duke if something were to happen to him. He pointed out that William was his closest living relative and therefore was the logical person to be his heir. The dukes of Normandy were vassals of the king of France, and Robert let his nobles know that he had asked the king, Henry I, to give official approval for William to become his heir. The king had agreed to Robert's request.

WILLIAM BECOMES DUKE OF NORMANDY

Robert now asked the Norman nobles to also agree to let William be his heir, to become duke if anything happened to him. He explained that he would appoint some of his relatives and best friends to be William's guardians— his cousin, Count Alan of Brittany, Archbishop Robert, of the city of Rouen; a young man named Osbern Crepon, to be the caretaker of William's lands and castles; and a man known as Turchetil, to be William's tutor. All these people would help William carry out the duties of a duke until he was old enough to take over himself. There was some reluctance, but most of the nobles finally agreed to recognize William as Robert's heir, and swore allegiance to him.

With William now taken care of, Robert apparently wanted to see that William's mother, Arlette, would also be secure. Before he left on his pilgrimage, he arranged for one of his nobles, a man named Herluin, to marry her. With everything now apparently in order, Robert began his journey. He took with him twenty knights and many servants. In keeping with his image as a magnificent person, he rode a mule that wore horseshoes of solid gold.[1] Hoofed animals always lost their shoes after a time, leaving them on roads and paths. Robert may have intended these costly shoes to become valuable gifts from him to whoever might find them.

This regional flag of Normandy shows two lions passant guardunt (in heraldry these are known as leopards rather than lions).

A year later, in 1035, word came that Duke Robert had died of disease somewhere in present-day Turkey. At the age of about eight, William was suddenly Duke of Normandy.

LIFE FOR AN EIGHT-YEAR-OLD DUKE

What was it like for an eight-year-old to be a duke, nearly a thousand years ago?

For one thing, being a noble, William ate a great deal better than the children of peasants, laborers, or most other commoners. For many of those people, the main food was bread, made from wheat, rye, and other grains, ground into flour, mixed with water, and baked. Most commoners seldom ate meat, and some never got to eat it. William would have eaten a great deal of meat—roasted or stewed beef, pork, sheep, goat, deer, rabbit, squirrel, chicken, duck, goose, and several other kinds of birds, including crows. He would have also had bacon, sausage, smoked and salted meat, and salted fish, chiefly herring.

Milk was drunk only by peasants, generally straight from the cow. It was mainly made into cheese and butter. So, unlike children of today, William probably did not know what milk tasted like. Water was generally considered bad and in most cases it was, depending on where it came from, so most people did not drink water, unless it came from a spring known to be pure. There were no fruit juices available. William would have drunk weak ale, a type of beer made from grain boiled in water, and wine, diluted with boiled water.

There was no such thing as candy, for sugar was unknown in Western Europe in the 1000s. The only "sweet" was honey, and William was probably occasionally given the treat of a honeycomb to chew on. William most likely ate fresh fruit such as cherries, raspberries, and strawberries, in season, and dried fruit, such as raisins, prunes, and apples, in winter.

The clothing of common people was made of wool, sheared from sheep, and linen, a cloth made from the stems of a plant called flax. William probably wore some clothing made of these cloths, too, but his clothing would have been better made than that of commoners. He would also have had robes made of bear skin, ermine, and other furred animals, to keep him warm in winter, and he would have worn short boots made of leather. He might also have had some garments made of silk, from far-off China, which could only be afforded by people of wealth, such as dukes.

THE YOUNG DUKE LEARNS TO LIVE WITH DANGER

As the ruler of Normandy, William was wealthy, owned castles and a vast amount of land, ate very well, was well-dressed, and was kept comfortable. He should have had an easy, happy life. However, his life actually became filled with dread and danger.

In the period of history sometimes known as the Dark Ages, when William lived, nearly every country or region in Europe was ruled by a nobleman—king, prince, duke, count, baron, or earl. Even though these people had great power and wealth, their lives were rarely easy and far from safe. There were usually many people, often even members of their own families, who longed to take their place, and were perfectly willing to kill them, or have them killed, to do so! Kings, princes, dukes, and other nobles were poisoned, stabbed to death, or killed in other ways, sometimes by family members, sometimes even by brothers or sons. William's own father, Robert, was believed by many people to have murdered his older brother by poison, in order to become duke of Normandy.[2]

William was surrounded by people who were not willing to accept him as their ruler and wanted to take his place, and others who wanted to control him in order to have power for themselves. He had uncles and cousins who believed they had a great deal more right to be duke of Normandy than a little boy whose mother had been a commoner. There were also others, not even related to William, who wanted to be duke. Some of these men had no concern at all about removing the young boy from their path by killing him. Nor did they have any concern about killing each other to get what they wanted. The exact thing that many Normans had feared when Duke Robert had announced he was going on a pilgrimage now happened. When William became duke, quarrels, feuds, and actual warfare broke out among many of the noble families of Normandy. There were battles and murders.

AN ATTEMPT ON WILLIAM'S LIFE

People who wanted to gain control of William began trying to get rid of the people who were taking care of him. When William was eleven, Count Alan died suddenly, possibly from poison. His place as William's guardian was taken by Count Gilbert of Brionne, who had been another friend of William's father. However, just a few months later, Count Gilbert was murdered by assassins while he was out hunting, and soon after that, Turchetil was also assassinated. A relative of William's known as Ralph of Gace, who had ordered the assassination of Count Gilbert, and perhaps of Turchetil as well, made himself William's guardian.

Then, someone who simply wanted William out of the way in order to take his place made a move. Some assassins, hired by an unknown person to murder the boy, managed to creep into the room in Castle Vaudreuil where William was sleeping one summer night. William was not alone in the room, Osbern Crepon was asleep in another bed. As it chanced, the assassins noticed his form lying in the bed before they saw William. Thinking he was William, one of the men savagely plunged a dagger into Crepon's body. Crepon may have let out a shriek of pain and shock as he died, William may have awakened and yelled for help. At any rate, William's guards came rushing into the room with torches and drawn swords and the murderers were cut down before they could kill the boy.

WILLIAM GOES INTO HIDING

Obviously, William was not safe, and his Uncle Walter, his mother's brother, took him into hiding. Walter often hid him in the huts of poor peasant families, where William's enemies would never have thought to look. For a time, no one but William's most trusted guardians knew where he was.

Nothing is really known of William's life at this time in his childhood, but many things can be reasoned out. He was probably living with his mother and her husband, Herluin. Herluin was a noble with the rank of viscount, and he owned a great amount of land, a large house, horses, and servants. He probably also employed a small force of soldiers. He would have been able to protect William against people who meant him harm.

What could the boy's life have been like? Were there any children who were his friends and playmates? We know that his mother had two sons with Herluin, who were named Odo and Robert. Thus, William had two half-brothers. He also had two half-sisters, one whose name was Adelaide, and the other whose name is unknown. He must have spent time with these children, but they were all younger than he. Did he have any friends of his own age? We know of one, a boy named William fitz Osbern. This was the son of Osbern Crepon who was killed by the assassins who had sneaked into Vaudreuil Castle to try to kill Duke William. The two Williams were the best of friends all their lives.

A Hidden Duke in Normandy

AT THE POINT IN HIS LIFE WHEN WILLIAM WAS
more or less in hiding, things were happening in England
that were going to be of great importance to his future.

England, at the time of William's childhood, was
broken up into four districts called earldoms—
Northumbria, Wessex, Mercia, and East Anglia. These
were ruled by noblemen called earls, like the counts of
Normandy and France. The earldoms were formed of a
number of small districts called shires, governed by men
known as shire-reeves (from which we get the word
"sheriff"). The whole country was ruled by a king, Cnut,
but there was also a "Great Council," called by the Old
English word *Witan*, that met to make important
decisions. One of the most important decisions they had
to make, from time to time, was choosing who would
be king.

Edward and Alfred, the sons of Ethelred, the last
Anglo-Saxon king of England, were grown men, living at
the court of William's father, Duke Robert, when William

was born. Edward was now regarded by many people in England as the lawful heir to the English throne. Duke Robert was their cousin, and was said to have been as fond of them as if they had been his brothers. There is some evidence that he even intended to try an invasion of England at one time, to help them regain their kingdom, but this did not come about. It is certain that they and William knew each other when he was a young child, but it is doubtful they had much to do with one another because of their age difference.

THE HORRIBLE DEATH OF PRINCE ALFRED

Most of the information we have about events in England during the time of Duke William of Normandy comes from a written account known as the *Anglo-Saxon Chronicle*. This is a group of seven manuscripts that cover about eleven centuries of the history of England, to the year 1154. It was written in Old English by several generations of monks working in monasteries and cathedrals in many parts of England. It consists of short descriptions of the major events of one year after another, although not all years are covered. Some of the things that William did in Normandy are described in the *Chronicle*, but the descriptions do not always agree with what Norman historians had to say.

In 1035, the year William became duke of Normandy, Cnut died and his son, Harold, known as Harold Harefoot, became king. A year later, Prince Alfred sailed from Normandy to England to visit his mother, Emma. One of the most powerful men in England at this time was Edwin Godwine, earl of the vast region known as Wessex. One of his sons, Harold, was earl of East Anglia, another son, Sweyn, ruled a territory made up of several shires. Edwin was a supporter of King Harold Harefoot, and it may be that he and King Harold schemed to do away with Prince Alfred. After all, Alfred was a son of the last Anglo-Saxon king of England, Ethelred, and therefore he had a strong claim to the throne of England. There were many Anglo-Saxons who would rather have had an Anglo-Saxon king than a Danish one. Thus, Alfred was a threat to Harold Harefoot.

Soon after Alfred arrived in England, Edwin Godwine and a group of his men attacked Alfred and the Normans who were guarding him. They killed most of the guards, seized Alfred, and turned him over to a group of King Harold's soldiers. These men blinded the prince, probably by poking red-hot irons into his eyes, then took him to a monastery to be looked after by the monks. He soon died. Horrible as this sounds, it was not at all unusual, at that time, for people in power to use such a way to get rid of someone they thought was a threat.

PRINCE EDWARD BECOMES KING OF ENGLAND

Harold Harefoot died in 1040 and his half-brother, Harthacnut, became king. While Harold and Harthacnut had the same father, they had different mothers, and

Harthacnut's mother was none other than Emma, the mother of Edward, Alfred, and their sister, Goda. Therefore, Harthacnut was the half-brother of Emma's other remaining son, Edward, who was still living in Normandy. Harthacnut had no children, so the logical heir to the throne was his closest living relative, Edward. In 1041, probably at the urging of the Witan, Harthacnut invited Edward to come to England to be officially named as Harthacnut's successor—the man who would become king if Harthacnut died.

In the summer of 1042 Harthacnut died suddenly at the age of twenty-five. The Witan quickly met and announced that Edward would be the next king of England. He was crowned king in early spring 1043, the year Duke William of Normandy became fifteen years old. He became known as Edward the Confessor, probably because he was very religious.

Thus, while William was in hiding in Normandy, his relative Edward was ruling England. They were in two vastly different situations and probably never even thought about each other, but they were linked together in a way that was going to greatly change the future of their two countries.

FEUDS, BATTLES, AND CASTLES

While William was in hiding, the feuding and quarrels between nobles continued and even grew worse. Many of these people built special dwellings in which they could more easily defend themselves and which they could use as bases from which to attack their enemies. These were the first kind of castles. They were square buildings sitting on artificial hills made of piled-up earth, with high wooden walls around them. Most had a deep ditch or moat around the wall, generally filled with water. The building had two stories, but there was no door or entrance in the bottom story—a person entered through the story above, by means of a trap door and ladder. The entrance to the building was on the second story. It was a slanted drawbridge that could be lowered across the moat. At first the buildings were made of wood, and they were cramped and crowded, with few rooms, but this was how many nobles lived, to be safe

The Normans were known for their strong stone castles.

from other nobles. In time, the wooden buildings were rebuilt of stone. Normandy became a land of castles.

It was not only nobles who became involved in battles with each other. Many peasants also became drawn into the squabbles and feuds of noble families, but while the nobles were fighting to gain more wealth and power, the peasants were simply trying to protect their families, their farms, and their means of making a living. When the sons of one count attempted to cause trouble for one of their father's enemies by damaging the farms and crops of his peasants, the peasants rose up and fought them. The sons and some of their soldiers were captured and executed. Events of this sort happened in a number of provinces. In some places, the leaders of the peasants were parish priests, who were so outraged by the actions of nobles that they convinced the peasants to rise up and defend themselves.

WORKERS, WORSHIPPERS, AND FIGHTERS

As Duke of Normandy, William was also a noble, of much higher rank than Herluin. Herluin was actually William's vassal, a man who owed him loyalty and obedience. Herluin had been a close friend of William's father, Robert, and probably felt he also owed the little boy some of the things his father would have given him. One of these would have been training in how to *be* a noble.

William's world was made up of three kinds of people: those who worked, those who prayed, and those who fought. The workers were people who produced things. They were people such as farmers, bakers, and winemakers, who produced food; and carpenters, weavers, metalworkers, leather makers, and others who produced things people needed, such as furniture, tools, leather, and cloth.

Those who prayed were the monks, priests, and nuns. Their major duty was to provide all people with help and favor from God, by means of prayer and religious ceremonies. They were also the record keepers, as they were the people with the ability to read and write.

Those who fought were the nobles. It was regarded as their duty to fight for the land if it was invaded by an enemy, or to fight to gain land from an enemy by invading his territory. Thus, as a noble, William had to be taught how to fight. This included not only actual hand-to-hand fighting with weapons, but also leadership, for nobles were the commanders of the common soldiers in a battle. We can be sure that William was taught to be skillful with weapons, taught to be a skillful horseman, taught how to choose the best ground for a battle and how to put a force of soldiers in the best position, and taught how to take care of an army. He probably spent most of his days, for several years, learning all these things. Herluin would have been able to teach him a great deal, for he had fought in battles with William's father.

WILLIAM COMES OUT OF HIDING

William came out of hiding as a teenager, but he was still in danger, and there were people who refused to accept him as duke. When he was thirteen or fourteen, a nobleman named Thurman Goz seized control of the Norman city of Falaise, and announced that Falaise was no longer part of Normandy—not part of William's realm. William apparently felt that if he were to give in and ignore this he would lose all respect. With Ralph of Gace commanding the small number of soldiers William had to follow him, he marched to Falaise. Once there, William called upon the people to support him. To his delight, men came to him by the hundreds and he led an attack on Falaise castle, where Goz was staying. As William's force broke into the castle, Goz fled, and left Normandy forever.

Apparently when he was about fifteen William was sent to live for a time at the court of the king of France, Henry I. The court of a king was made up of many people, mostly all nobles, who acted as the king's advisors and assistants. Many of them had actual duties to perform. There was a treasurer, who looked after expenses, a steward, who looked after the king's eating arrangements and food, and so on. The court did not always stay in one place, but often moved around the country with the king, staying in the castles or manor houses of nobles for a time. In each region he visited, the king might check to see if laws were being properly enforced, and look after other things that involved government.

It was common for young nobles who were vassals of the king, as William was, to live with the court for a while. It was a way for the king to find out what sort of men they were becoming. At some time while William was at Henry's court, the king made him a knight. This was done in a special ceremony, and it was a high point in the life of any young noble.

After a few years William returned to Normandy and increasingly took on more of a duke's duties. But in 1046, when William was about eighteen, a full-scale revolt broke out against him, led by his cousin Guy of Burgundy and a group of nobles. These men were determined to replace William with Guy, and they intended to kill William to do it.

A Battle
and a Siege

WILLIAM MUST HAVE KNOWN THAT A REBELLION was brewing, but perhaps he did not take it seriously enough at first. Like most young noblemen of that time, William enjoyed hunting, and this almost cost him his life. One day he rode to a castle called Valognes, to spend a day hunting in the forest that surrounded the castle. Rather foolishly, he did not bring any soldiers with him. One of the supporters of Guy of Burgundy happened to be staying nearby with a large force of armed followers. Someone brought him word that William was at Valognes, alone, and he began gathering his troops together to ride there.

Somehow, William learned of his danger. According to a story that has come down through time, there was a man by the name of Gallet with the rebel force, who was a jester—a clown who made his living by entertaining people with jokes, tricks, and juggling. This man was loyal to William. Realizing what was happening, he set out for Valognes at a dead run, reached it before Guy's supporters arrived, and warned William. Most historians think this story was simply made up, but whatever happened, William had time to leave the castle on horseback, and rode away at breakneck speed through the countryside. At Valognes, the rebel group spent time searching the castle for William, which probably prevented them from catching up to him and putting him to death.

According to the story, William managed to cross a rising river just in time, before it got too high, and reached the town of Ryes where Hubert, the Lord of Ryes, was one of his supporters. Hubert provided William with a fresh horse, and sent him off with his three sons to protect him. When the rebels arrived at Ryes, Hubert sent them off in the wrong direction. William eventually reached Falaise, a place where he was among people who would protect him from his enemies. The rebels soon gave up the chase.

William the Conqueror would one day wear a king's crown. But first he had a long road of battles before him.

THE KING OF FRANCE COMES TO WILLIAM'S AID

William must have decided there was only one thing for him to do. He went to King Henry, and asked the king to help him. In 1031, when William was about three years old, Henry had been faced with a revolt headed by his own mother. He fled into Normandy, looking for help. William's father, Duke Robert, had brought the small Norman army to reinforce the king's army, and helped him defeat the rebellion. Henry apparently felt he owed William something because William's father had once helped him. Henry came riding into Normandy with an army of about three thousand men, to help William defeat the rebellion. William met him with a small force of Norman knights who were loyal to him.

The army of William and King Henry met the rebel force on a rolling open plain called Val-ès-Dune, between the cities of Falaise and Rouen, in January 1047. Apparently both armies consisted of only armored knights on horseback, with no foot soldiers or archers. Thus, the battle that took place was just a matter of knights riding at each other and slashing away with their swords. According to written accounts of the battle, by men who lived at the time, Duke William showed that he was a brave and fierce fighter. A man known as William of Poitiers wrote that Duke William hurled himself against his enemies and "terrified them with slaughter."[1] He rode against a famous and feared warrior by the name of Hardez of Bayeux, and killed him with a vicious sword blow. Apparently, William, like many young men, was rather reckless about exposing himself to danger, and King Henry later scolded him for not being more cautious.[2]

After a time, the rebels began to lose heart. Some of them retreated, riding away from the battle. Then, suddenly, the entire rebel force collapsed, galloping full speed to the rear. But their fighting position had been badly chosen—a river lay behind them. Hundreds of men and horses were drowned trying to get across it. It was said that the river became so choked with bodies that the wheels of water mills along the bank were unable to turn.[3]

WILLIAM WINS HIS FIRST SIEGE

The rebel army that Guy of Burgundy had led against William no longer existed, but Guy was still a problem. Although wounded in the Battle of Val-ès Dunes, he had escaped from the battlefield with a large number of men and shut himself up in his castle of Brionne. Brionne was a stone building with a wall around it, on an island in the middle of a river called the Risle, and it was a strong fortress. However, William knew that he had to capture it. He could not risk having an enemy sitting in the middle of Normandy who might be able to come out and attack him the minute his back was turned.

William took his army to Brionne. He tried to take it by storm, with his men battering at the gates and climbing the walls on ladders. This failed. William saw that he would have to put the castle under siege. That meant keeping the castle surrounded so that no one could get in or out, and waiting for the people inside to run out of food. William had his men put up wooden fences and towers, from which his archers could pour arrows into anyone trying to break out of the castle. It took three years, but Guy finally begged to surrender. William allowed Guy's followers to come trudging out of the castle and go wherever they wished, but Guy was ordered out of Normandy and forbidden to ever return. Brionne became William's castle.

WILLIAM IMPOSES A "TRUCE OF GOD"

In October 1047, some seven months after the Battle of Val-ès-Dunes, William called together a meeting of the top officials of the Christian Church in Normandy at the town of Caen. With their assistance, he proclaimed what was called a Truce of God throughout the dukedom. This meant that all quarrels, feuds, and warfare of any kind between noble families, were absolutely forbidden by the Church from Wednesday evening until Monday morning, and during the entire time in the seasons of Advent, Lent, Easter, and Pentecost. Anyone breaking the truce would be excommunicated—shut out of all activities of the Church. This was, and still is, the worst punishment the Catholic Church can inflict. Most people of William's time would never have dared risk having it happen to them.

The Truce meant that nobles such as Guy of Burgundy would no longer be able to put together an army of rebellion. On the other hand, William, as duke, had the authority to keep an army together in order to protect the duchy against invasion or against any problem that might rise within it. He had the ability to enforce peace within Normandy. The Norman peasants, who suffered badly during rebellions, hailed the Truce of God with great joy.

The Battle of Val-ès-Dunes was a great victory for William, but he was still far from secure as duke, and the battle was not the end of the fighting he faced.

A Wife Is Chosen for William

One of the greatest concerns to people of the Middle Ages, ruled by kings and dukes, was that their ruler had a successor, a person who would become ruler when the present ruler died. The successor could be a brother, or even a cousin or uncle, but generally people preferred that it be a son. For that reason, everyone wanted their ruler to be married. William was not yet married, so some time after the Battle of Val-ès-Dunes, the nobles of Normandy began looking around for a suitable wife for him.

Marriages, especially those of nobles, were handled very differently at that time than they are today. Marriages were generally arranged like a business deal, between the fathers of a man and woman. William's father was dead, so some Norman noblemen took his place. The main purpose of a marriage of two nobles was to make an alliance between their two countries or provinces. It did not matter whether or not the man and woman even knew each other. William's wife had to be a noble, of course, and had to come from a place that had a strong army, but it did not matter what she looked like, how smart she was, or anything else of that sort. What was important to the Norman nobles was that William get married as soon as possible, gain a good alliance, and start having children.

The nobles finally settled on a girl named Matilda, daughter of Count Baldwin of Flanders, which is now part of the nation of Belgium. It was then a strong and wealthy region that would be a powerful ally for Normandy. Matilda was about seventeen years old, and a very tiny girl, only a little more than four feet tall.[4] Matilda was said to be pretty and clever. William was willing to marry her.

A MARRIAGE AGREEMENT

There is a very old story from Normandy, that when Matilda heard that William was being considered as a husband for her, she refused. She felt that he was beneath her because his mother had been a commoner. According to the story, William became so angry when he heard this that he burst into Matilda's room and actually slapped and even kicked her. The story maintains that this treatment somehow changed her mind and made her insist that William was now the only man she would ever consider marrying!

Most historians doubt that anything such as this actually happened. But it may have, for a story has to come from something. There are many stories, known to be true, of nobles mistreating their wives. If it did happen, it tells us that William must have had a fiery temper, and perhaps did not allow anything to stand in his way. At any rate, the marriage was agreed to.

At the time of the marriage agreement, William was probably at his full height and best appearance. It is known that he was about five feet, ten-inches tall, which was fairly tall for a man then, when people were considerably smaller than they are now. An average size adult man was about five feet, five inches, much smaller than many teenagers of today. Descriptions of William say that he was somewhat burly and had gray eyes and reddish-brown hair, and thin lips. A monk, who lived at the same time as William and knew him slightly, wrote of him, "He was great in body and strong, tall in stature but not ungainly."[5] His voice was said to be guttural—harsh and throaty. We do not know what William's face looked like, for there are no paintings of him from that time now in existence, only some small, simple, embroidered pictures. They show that apparently he did not wear a beard as some men did then.

WILLIAM'S PERSONALITY

What sort of a person was William? At that time it was quite common for nobles to overeat and to drink so much wine and ale that they often became drunk. However, the monk who wrote about William said that he was "temperate in eating and drinking. Especially was he moderate in drinking, for he abhorred drunkenness in all men."[6] Some of the tales told about him, such as the one concerning his beating of Matilda, seem to show that he had a vicious temper. He was apparently a very religious

41

person. The monk who described him said, "He followed the Christian discipline in which he had been brought up as a child, and whenever his health permitted he regularly and with great piety [reverence] attended Christian worship each morning and evening, and at the celebration of Mass."[7]

With Guy gone from Normandy and no other rebels causing any trouble, William was now firmly in control of Normandy. As duke, William had many powers he could make use of as he wished. One of those powers was that he controlled all the activities of the Church in his dukedom. All archbishops, bishops, priests, and monks were his vassals, like the counts and viscounts, and he could appoint them or dismiss them. Some time between October 1049, and April 1050, he made his half-brother, Odo, bishop of Bayeux, a city in northern Normandy. Odo was only about nineteen years old at the time. It was a very high position for such a young man.

FIRST CONQUEST

ONCE HE BECAME THE ESTABLISHED DUKE OF Normandy, William began leading the armies and fighting the battles that would turn Normandy into a major power of Europe. The armies that William commanded and those he fought against were something new in Europe at this time. Most European armies were made up mainly of foot soldiers, men who fought on foot, armed with swords or spears. However in France and particularly in Normandy, a new kind of soldier had appeared, a soldier who fought on horseback, wearing full armor. These were the soldiers who have become known as knights. In Normandy and France, at William's time, they were known by the French word *chevalier*, meaning horseman.

The knights were specially trained fighting men. They learned to be skilled riders before the age of twelve, because it was said that after that, a boy would only be fit to be a priest.[1] Knights learned special ways of using their weapons on horseback. The stirrups that hung from their saddles were long enough so that a knight could sit with his legs hanging straight. This enabled him to actually stand in the stirrups and swing his sword or thrust his lance with the full force of his body. Thus, a charge of Norman knights was like an onrushing avalanche that *smashed* into an enemy force, throwing its men in all directions, trampling them, thrusting spear points through them, slicing them with sword cuts that opened up bodies and took off hands, arms, and heads! A medieval historian said that a charge of French and Norman knights could knock a hole through the wall of a city![2]

COUNT GEOFFREY, "THE HAMMER," MAKES A THREATENING MOVE

The first war that Duke William and his knights fought for Normandy was against a neighbor. Normandy was surrounded by provinces of France, ruled by French counts. The province just to the south of Normandy was called Maine, and just south of Maine was the province of Anjou. Technically, all provinces, including Normandy, were under the rule of the King of France, Henry, and the counts or dukes who ruled them were all his vassals. However, most provinces were ruled by men who did pretty much as they wanted to do, even as far as going to war with another province and trying to take it over.

The province of Anjou was ruled by an ambitious, greedy, warlike count, named Geoffrey Martel. His nickname was "the Hammer"—Geoffrey the Hammer. When the count of Maine died in 1051, Count Geoffrey

44

This Norman knight carries a lance and a kite-shaped shield.
The shield protected the knight from neck to ankle. He used
his lance to stab at enemy horsemen. During closer combat,
he used a sword.

THE KNIGHTS OF NORMANDY

The Norman knights wore body armor and cone-shaped helmets with a strip of metal that hung down to cover their nose. The body armor was called mail. It was made of rows of metal rings, each ring linked to the ring above, below, and on each side of it. Thus, the rows of rings could move. This made the armor flexible, so a man could move all parts of his body while wearing it. The mail was made into coats, with sleeves that reached to just below the elbow, and skirts that reached to the calves of the legs. The skirts were split, so that the man in the armor could sit on a horse. These coats of armor were called hauberks, and a *hauberk* weighed about thirty-two pounds. They were worn over shirtlike garments that were probably padded.

The knights carried a long kite-shaped shield that covered them on one side of the body from neck to ankle. Their weapons were a sword and a twelve-foot long lance, or spear. Their horses, too, were actually weapons. They were trained to rear up and lash out with their hooves against the enemies they charged. They were taught to trample on men in their path, and even to bite!

A knight's mail armor had to be made by hand by skilled, experienced men, so it took a long time to make, and was costly. Warhorses were specially bred and trained over a long period of time by men who were experts, so a well-trained warhorse was very expensive. Even a knight's sword was specially made by men skilled in the art of sword-making. It was expensive to be a knight, and most knights were nobles or sons of nobles, with some wealth.

of Anjou marched an army into Maine and occupied its capital city, Le Mans. This gave him control of the whole province.

At the border between Maine and Normandy was a narrow strip of hilly land known as Bellême, which belonged to a noble family by that name. It contained two fortified towns, called Domfront and Alençon. Geoffrey marched north and occupied both towns. Alençon was right at the border of Normandy, and a road led through it straight to Duke William's main stronghold of Falaise. It looked very much as if Count Geoffrey was threatening an invasion of Normandy.

WILLIAM MARCHES AGAINST "THE HAMMER"

William could certainly not ignore such a threat. As quickly as possible, he formed an army. This was done by sending messages to all his vassals who were sworn to fight for him in time of war, telling them they were needed and where to meet. The counts, barons, and other vassals quickly made arrangements to see that their lands would be looked after while they were gone. They had their swords and spears sharpened and oiled, their shields repaired as necessary, and their armor cleaned. Spare clothing and provisions, such as dry hard sausage and cheese, were packed into small horse-drawn wagons. Mounted on their warhorses, followed by the knights who were their vassals, and with a few retainers who would serve as foot soldiers, the nobles set out to where the duke waited. In early autumn 1051, William marched his army into Bellême and headed toward Domfront. Geoffrey quickly moved to meet him.

An account written at the time tells that Geoffrey and William sent messengers to each other, describing the colors and designs of their shields, so they could recognize each other on the battlefield. At that time, leaders of armies sometimes settled a battle by fighting a single combat against each other, and perhaps that is what William and Geoffrey intended to do. However, apparently a full-scale battle was fought instead. Almost nothing is known about it, but the result of it seems to have been that Geoffrey retreated, and eventually pulled completely out of Maine back into Anjou. William and his Normans must have been victorious.

WILLIAM USES CRUELTY TO WIN A VICTORY

William continued to Domfront, but the town did not welcome him. Apparently its citizens and soldiers were loyal to the Bellême family and were unwilling to surrender the town to Normans. It stayed shut up tight, and William put it under siege. However, as the siege stretched through the winter into 1052, he became unwilling to let it continue any longer, and came up with a scheme. One night, he left part of his army spread out around the town, with many camp fires burning so it would look as if the whole army were still there. Then, under cover of the darkness, William took the rest on a fast march to Alençon, thirty miles away. They arrived at dawn. There was a small fort across the river from the town, and William called on the soldiers who were defending it to surrender. They refused, and shouted insults at him. Leading his men forward he took the fort by storm, slaughtering most of the defenders and taking about thirty prisoners. To make sure everyone in Bellême understood they could not defy him, he had his soldiers inflict horrible punishment on the captives—their hands and feet were cut off. This was a horribly cruel thing to do, but actually, William was not being any crueler than most any other nobleman of his time. Punishments of that sort, to strike terror in people, were quite common in the Middle Ages. Terrified, the people of Alençon surrendered their town. William saw to it that the people of Domfront learned of what had been done at Alençon, and they, too, soon offered to surrender. Bellême was conquered, and it was now part of Normandy.

A GOOD MARRIAGE

At some time between 1050 and 1052, between besieging fortresses, William and Matilda were married. For reasons that are unknown now, their marriage was forbidden by Pope Leo IX. It may be that he believed they were distantly related because they may have both been descended from Duke Rollo. They ignored the pope's command not to marry. The exact date of the marriage is not known.

At that time, most kings, dukes, and other noblemen did not pay much attention to their wives, preferring to pay attention to other women. William's own father, Duke Robert, had even sent his wife away for good before he met Arlette, the girl who became William's mother. However, it seems clear that William remained true to Matilda throughout their entire marriage. William and his wife really seemed to be quite fond of each other. Over a number of years they had a large amount of children. The exact number is not actually known, but there were at least eight and possibly ten. There were four sons—Robert, Richard, William, and Henry. There were also at least four daughters, whose names may have been Agatha, Constance, Adela, and Cecily, but there may have been two others, Adeliza and Matilda. The dates of birth of only two of the sons are known, and none of the daughters' birthdays are known. Such things were not considered important then, and careful records were not kept.

KING HENRY TURNS AGAINST WILLIAM

It was known throughout Normandy that Duke William's uncle, Count William of the district of Talou in Normandy, believed that he should have been made Duke of Normandy and resented his nephew. However, he was with William in Bellême, commanding part of the Norman forces and helping at the siege of Domfront. He seemed to be supporting Duke William. Suddenly, for an unknown reason, he simply left one night and rode back into Normandy. He closed himself up in his powerful castle overlooking the town of Arques and let it be known that he no longer was willing to give obedience to Duke William.

As soon as Duke William learned that he had another rebellion on his hands he acted quickly. He set out with only a few men but was soon joined by other loyal followers. When they reached the castle at Arques they found a number of Count William's followers waiting for them, prepared to fight. There was a short battle and the count's men took refuge in the castle. Duke William decided he would have to conduct yet another siege.

The takeover of Bellême had seemed a triumph for William, but it was actually going to be the cause of some serious trouble for him. King Henry of France apparently became worried by William's victory over the Count of Anjou. It may have seemed to the king that the young Duke of Normandy was becoming a little too powerful. At any rate, Henry, who had knighted William and fought at his side in the Battle of Val-ès-Dunes, now turned against him. It may be that Count William made some kind of a deal with King Henry, but whatever the reason, Henry decided to support him against Duke William. In the autumn of 1053 Henry came riding into Normandy at the head of a French army, to help Count William overthrow his nephew as Duke of Normandy.

FACING A FULL-SCALE WAR

It was the king's intention to bring fighting men and provisions to Count William in his castle. However, Duke

William was not caught napping. He had learned a French army was coming and had moved quickly once again. The king was shocked to find a Norman army in position blocking his movement to the castle. When he tried to slip a large force of troops around the Normans to reach the castle, a section of Duke William's army ambushed them and wiped them out. Hundreds of Frenchmen went down under a hail of Norman arrows, and the wagons of provisions that were being brought to the castle were captured.

King Henry apparently decided he would not be able to get any help to Count William. He pulled his army out of Normandy and took it back to France. Duke William's siege of Arques castle continued until the gaunt and starving defenders sent a message to William asking for terms of surrender. He was surprisingly merciful, allowing them to come trudging out without punishment. However, Count William was ordered out of Normandy, never to return.

The sieges of Brionne, Domfront, and Arques, were highpoints in Duke William's early military career. He had shown that he was a master at conducting sieges and winning them. However, even though William had now put down another rebellion and gained a fine new castle, he faced a major problem. King Henry could not allow a man who was supposedly his vassal defy him. Normandy was now in a full-scale war with the kingdom of France!

A Rebellion in England

IN ENGLAND, IN THE YEARS WHEN WILLIAM WAS fighting rebellions and trying to remain duke, King Edward was having a struggle with Edwin Godwine, the Earl of Wessex, over who would run the kingdom. Godwine quickly began trying to get control of Edward. In 1045 he pushed Edward into marrying his daughter Edith, which Edward apparently did not particularly want to do. Godwine probably hoped that Edith would have a baby boy who some day would become king. That would give Godwine's family even greater power—they would be the family of a king.

It is very likely that Edward hated Godwine for his part in the blinding and death of Edward's brother, Alfred. Edward may also have felt that he was not safe with Godwine having so much power, and apparently decided he had better have some people around him he could trust. Edward began bringing friends he had made in Normandy to England, and giving them land and putting them in positions of importance. Some of these men built Norman-style castles on their land, which is how castles came to England.

In 1051, while Duke William was busy besieging Domfront, Edward's sister Goda came to England with her husband, Eustace, the French count of Boulogne, to visit her brother. They came on a French ship, with a French and Norman crew and a guard of French knights. The ship docked at the English port city of Dover, which was in Godwine's earldom. Apparently, a riot broke out between some of the citizens of Dover and the French knights. Twenty people were killed. The count protested to King Edward. Edward sent an order to Godwine to punish the city of Dover by harrying it, which meant burning houses and hanging people. Godwine refused.

GODWINE AND FAMILY ARE EXILED FROM ENGLAND

To refuse a command from the king was rebellion, and apparently Godwine intended to rebel. He may have thought he had the power to take the throne from Edward and become king himself. He put together a large army of men from his earldom as well as from the earldoms of his sons. Then he sent a demand to the king to turn Eustace and all the Frenchmen over to him for punishment.

King Edward also formed an army, with men supplied by the loyal earls of Northumbria and Mercia. England appeared to be on the verge of civil war—a war between its own people, divided against each other. As king, Edward had powers that gave him the upper hand. He issued a command for the army of England to come together. This meant that every able-bodied man in the country had to drop whatever he was doing and hurry to the place where Edward indicated the army should assemble. This was a command no Englishman could ignore. Godwine's army began to melt away as his men left to obey the king's call.

Godwine and his sons were ordered to come to London and stand trial before the Witan. Probably fearing that they would be seized and murdered before they arrived, they demanded to be given promises of safety. Edward coldly answered that they had five days to come to London, with no promises of any sort, or they would be made to leave the country.

Godwine and his family were beaten. Godwine and his wife, together with his sons Sweyn, Tostig, and Gyrth, and their families, sailed to Flanders. Harold Godwineson and his brother Leofwine and companions, sailed to Ireland. Even Godwine's daughter, Edith, Edward's wife, was banished in a way. Edward ordered her to leave the court, sending her to a nunnery to live, with only one female attendant to look after her instead of many, as queens usually had.

RUMOR ARISES THAT WILLIAM IS TO BE EDWARD'S HEIR

Now Edward was free to do as he wanted rather than let Godwine have his way. Having lived in Normandy so long, Edward had many Norman friends. He began bringing

Norman knights and clergymen to England in large groups, and giving them such high honors and positions that many Englishmen became annoyed. It was also about this time, in 1051 or 1052, that a belief began to grow that King Edward had promised to make Duke William of Normandy his heir—that William would become the king of England when Edward died.

There were a number of rumors about how this idea got started. One was that Edward had sent an invitation to William to come to England and see him. According to the story, which is in the Anglo-Saxon Chronicle, William came to England with a large group of Norman knights, probably in the spring of 1052, and met with the king, who told William of his decision to make William his heir. This was not likely however, for William was involved in besieging a number of fortresses in Normandy and Belême in the years 1051 and 1052. As the commander in charge of such important operations, he could never have gone away at such a time.

Another story suggested that William had sent a high-ranking Norman noble to England to see Edward, and the king told the nobleman of his decision. Still another story was that Edward had sent the archbishop of Canterbury to tell William. It is true that the archbishop made a journey to Rome in 1051, and he could have stopped at Rouen, where William lived, on the way, but there is no actual record that he did so. Whatever the truth, William claimed he had been offered the throne of England, and many people in England and Normandy believed him. So did many people in other parts of Europe, including the pope.

CIVIL WAR THREATENS ENGLAND

It may have been because of the rumors about William becoming heir to the English throne that, in 1052, Godwine and his sons attempted to return to England. They were quite wealthy and managed to take a great deal of treasure with them when they left England, so they were well able to buy ships and hire soldiers. Godwine put together a small fleet of ships and sailed to the coast of what had been his earldom. He went ashore and did some talking to people. He found that many of his former allies still supported him and were angry with Edward for bringing so many Normans into England.

Harold Godwineson hired nine ships and a small force of Irish fighting men, and made a raid on an area of coast that belonged to Edward. Then the father and son combined their forces, built them up with men who flocked to support them, and sailed up the Thames River to London. Edward had forty ships and his household guard in London.

Godwine and Harold anchored their ships some distance away, and their soldiers encamped around them on the riverbank. Once again it looked as if civil war could break out. However, no one really wanted that. The bishop of Winchester began to carry messages back and forth between Edward and Godwine, and eventually the Witan came together to decide what to do to prevent war. It ruled that Godwine was innocent of all the charges that had caused him to be exiled.

Edward was humiliated. He was forced to return their earldoms to Godwine and the Godwinesons. He was forced to take his wife, Edith, back. Most of his Norman friends had to leave England, including an archbishop and a bishop.

A FRENCH ARMY INVADES NORMANDY

Godwine had won. But he did not enjoy his victory for very long. In April 1053, he died of a stroke. This left Harold Godwineson the most powerful man in England. As Godwine's heir, he became earl of vast, wealthy Wessex. He was tremendously popular. A great many people wanted him to be England's next king, and he, himself, probably wanted to be England's next king.

The year after Godwine died was the year that Duke William's war with France began. Henry, the French king, assembled a very large army of men from all over France, He divided it into two parts, one commanded by himself and one by his brother, Count Odo of Blois. In February 1054, he invaded Normandy from two directions, his force coming from the west and Odo's from the east.

As was usually the case in wars between kings, dukes, and counts at that time, it was the peasants, the poor common people, who suffered the worst. People whose farms and homes were in the path of an invading army were in a dreadful situation. If they were lucky, they might simply have all their possessions taken by invading soldiers, and some of them, especially women, would be mistreated. If they were unlucky, many of them would be slaughtered and their homes burned down. When people had warning of an approaching army, they generally tried to run away. They took as much as they could, piling possessions in horse- or ox-drawn wagons, and dragging cows, sheep, or goats along by ropes. They tried to put as much distance as they could between themselves and the oncoming invaders. If there was a forest nearby they might try to hide in it, although forests were generally carefully searched by enemy soldiers. Even when peasants were able to survive the passing of an army, they knew that when they returned to their homes, they might find nothing but smoking, burned-out ruins. Soldiers often burned things just for fun.

THE FRENCH ARE CAUGHT BY SURPRISE

William called for help from his people, and men flocked to him from all over Normandy. He was able to put together a force large enough to be divided in two to meet the two French armies. William led his troops against those commanded by King Henry, one of his loyal supporters, Robert the Count of Eu, led the eastern force against Odo. However, both of the Norman forces were outnumbered by the French troops they faced. William did not want to risk battle with them until he was able to get some advantage. His instructions to his commanders were to simply keep watch on the invaders until they did something that left them open to attack—and then strike hard!

The Frenchman Odo was apparently not a very skillful commander. He did not seem to think he would encounter any opposition, so he did not bother to take any precautions. When his force came to a little town called Mortemer, between two hills and surrounded by forest, he decided it would be a pleasant place to use as a base. The French soldiers took over the town, and then spent their days spreading out over the countryside in order to do as much robbing, kill as many people, and burn as many houses as possible. Odo apparently allowed them to spend their nights feasting, drinking, and amusing themselves without making much effort to guard against attack.

This was exactly the sort of thing William had told his commanders to take advantage of. Cautiously and quietly on a February night in 1054, Count Robert set his forces moving on hidden paths through the forest to converge on Mortemer from all sides. At a signal, the Normans came roaring into the town like a whirlwind, in what became known as the Battle of Mortemer.

THE FRENCH HEAD BACK INTO FRANCE

There is no actual record of the battle from the time it took place, but many years later a writer apparently pieced together a description of what happened from stories he had heard. According to him, it was not so much a battle as a massacre! He tells of drunken French soldiers staggering out of their sleeping places and being cut down by the swords of the Norman knights without mercy. Some of the houses in the town were set on fire, and French soldiers in them, too drunk to be aroused, died in the smoke and flames. Count Odo managed to escape from the town, but other French leaders were killed or captured. It was a stunning victory for Normandy and a tremendous boost for Duke William.

King Henry was horrified when he learned what had happened. He had lost half his army and he was in no position to stay in Normandy—he was now the one that was outnumbered! He hurriedly pulled his force out of the duchy, back into France.

By now, most of William's vassals, counts, and bishops were actually relatives or very close friends who could be completely counted on to support him. As for those few who were not, they were easy to dispose of. Some time in 1055, William took the county of Mortain away from the man who had been its count and gave it to his half brother, Robert. Robert was now Count of Mortain and William was now strong enough to do pretty much what he wanted in Normandy.

7

VICTORIES AND MYSTERIES

KING HENRY OF FRANCE HAD APPARENTLY BEEN sulking over his last defeat at Mortemer and decided it was an insult that had to be punished. In August 1057, he again invaded Normandy with an army that contained a large portion of troops belonging to William's old enemy, Geoffrey the Count of Anjou. The Frenchmen pushed northward toward the towns of Bayeux and Caen. Again, there was a great deal of killing and burning in the Norman countryside as they passed through. Once more, it was the poor and the peasants who suffered most.

William made no attempt to protect his people, but there was probably not much he could do anyway. Again, he was outnumbered, so he used the same plan he had used before. He kept his force away from the French, but watched their movements and waited for them to make a mistake. The mistake happened when they reached the Dives River near a town called Varaville. The French army was strung out over many miles, and laden down with loot and provisions they had taken from farms and villages. They began to cross the river at a ford—a place where the water was shallow enough for men to wade through. However, the crossing took so long that the tide rose in the river and about half of the army was unable to cross. It was halted in a long column stretched out on the road on the wrong side of the river. William was lurking nearby with the Norman army.

When his scouts brought word of what had happened, he struck instantly.

WILLIAM STRIKES WITH HIS CAVALRY

The part of the French army that was strung out and stranded on one side of the river was mainly the army's rear. It consisted of mostly foot soldiers and what was known as the baggage-train—the horse-drawn wooden wagons that carried the army's supplies. Most of the wagons carried food, such as bags of flour for baking bread, bundles of dry smoked sausages, and barrels of ale and wine. Some wagons carried shoes and pieces of clothing, for such things wore out quickly and soldiers needed replacements. Most of the wagons had cows, sheep, or goats tied to them, which had been taken from Norman farms the French had passed.

The foot soldiers carried spears or swords and had no armor or helmets. Now faced with a long wait for the river to go down so they could cross, they began trying to make themselves comfortable. Many sank down to sit cross-legged in the road; some lay down to try to catch a catnap. A few groups of men kindled small fires with which to cook foodstuffs they had stolen from farms or village shops. Wagon drivers climbed down from their seats to stretch their legs and walk about.

Suddenly, they all became aware of a sound.

It was a sound they knew, the rumble of many horses' hoofs. Heads turned sharply, and men leaped to their feet, staring into the distance. Coming down at them from behind the crest of a hill was row upon row of mounted men, their armor gleaming and their raised swords flashing in the sun. Duke William's Norman cavalry!

THE END OF THE WAR WITH FRANCE

Most of the French soldiers simply turned and began to run away, as hard and as fast as they could. They knew they had no chance against this armored onslaught galloping at them. Some headed for the river, hoping to swim to safety on the other side. A few strong swimmers made it, but with the river as high and fast as it was, most drowned.

In moments the Norman knights were among the running men. Standing in their stirrups they slashed down with their swords with all their might. SLASH—and a man went down with his back sliced open! SLASH—and a man's head was nearly severed from his body!

Behind the knights came the Norman foot soldiers and archers. Where groups of French soldiers had formed to try to defend themselves, the archers simply shot them down, and the foot soldiers moved in to finish off those who were only wounded. Foot soldiers swarmed into the wagons to look for any Frenchmen who might have tried to hide themselves.

Almost the entire portion of the French army that had not been able to cross the river was wiped out. On the opposite side of the river, King Henry's heart must have sank as he watched the destruction of a sizeable part of his army and the capture of his baggage-train. Once again he was forced to flee from Normandy with what remained of his army. The French army traveled along the river until a bridge was reached. Moving quickly, the French crossed the bridge and headed back through Normandy toward the safety of France. The Battle of Varaville as it came to be known, turned out to be the last battle of the Norman war with France.

MYSTERIOUS EVENTS IN ENGLAND

While William was literally fighting for his life and future in Normandy, something happened in England that seems to have been a complicated plot involving him. Throughout England it was generally thought that William had been chosen as King Edward the Confessor's successor. Suddenly, it was learned that there was another person with a far better claim to be Edward's successor than William had. This was another man named Edward, known as Edward the Exile, and he was King Edward's nephew! He was the son of Edmund, King Edward's older brother who had stayed in England to help fight the Danes when Edward, Alfred, and Goda had gone with their mother to Normandy. Thus, Edward the Exile was a genuine Anglo-Saxon prince. He had been living in Hungary for forty-one years, which was why he had the nickname of "the Exile." In 1054, a group of English officials headed by the bishop of Worcester, went to Hungary and asked Edward to come to England. It is not known who sent them, but it might have been someone who wanted him to make a claim for the throne of England, and block William from getting it.

Edward the Exile arrived in England some time in 1057. With him were his wife and three children, a son and two daughters. He was supposed to go and meet with King Edward, but something happened. Apparently, he died rather mysteriously, before ever reaching London. An English monk who lived at that time wrote about this event in the Anglo-Saxon Chronicle, saying, "We do not know for what reason it was brought about that he was not allowed to visit his kinsman, King Edward." This sounds very much as if Edward the Exile might have been sent away again. However, the next line states that it was ". . . a miserable fate and grievous to all the people that he so speedily ended his life after he came to England. . . ."[1]

Was he, perhaps, assassinated? Could this have been done by someone who wanted to eliminate Edward as a threat to William or Harold? Could Edward the Exile have been brought to England simply to have him killed? Might William or Harold have had a hand in this? We can never know, but with the death of Edward the Exile, Duke

William was certainly once again the only person considered to be the true successor to Edward the Confessor.

WILLIAM'S LONG STRUGGLE FINALLY ENDS

In 1059 the marriage of William and Matilda was finally approved by the pope, who was then Nicholas II. As penance for having married against the objections of the Church, William and Matilda each agreed to build a church in the Normandy city of Caen. These churches, St. Stephen's, built by William, and the church of the Holy Trinity, built by Matilda, still stand in Caen today after more than nine centuries.

In Normandy, after the Battle of Varaville, William may have felt King Henry would attempt another invasion some time, for he began strengthening places along the Normandy border where he felt they might occur, but nothing happened. He might even have thought about invading France, to try to end the problem with Henry once and for all. But when King Henry died in August 1060, the whole situation changed. Henry's young son, a child named Philip, became king, and the man that King Henry had named in his will to become Philip's guardian was none other than Count Baldwin of Flanders, Duke William's father-in-law. Thus, Normandy was no longer in any danger from France. William's position as Duke of Normandy was finally secure.

In 1062, William began to take steps to enlarge Normandy. In March of that year, Count Herbert of the province of Maine died. Herbert's young sister was engaged to someday marry William's oldest son Robert, who was then a boy of ten. When Herbert died, William demanded that Robert be given full possession of Maine. However, some of the most important nobles and citizens of Maine refused to agree to this. They announced that they wanted Walter of Mantes, the count of the province of Vexin, to become the new count of Maine. As always, William acted instantly. He sent a small portion of his army to cause trouble in Vexin and, with the rest, invaded Maine.

He headed straight for Maine's capital, the city of Le Mans. As was usual with a medieval invasion, William allowed his army to destroy all the crops, farms, and villages in its path. The purpose of this was to make the land around Le Mans desolate and wipe out all the sources of food that the capital city depended on. Thus, William would not have to try to take Le Mans by storm, risking his troops; he was actually putting the city under siege and working to starve it into surrendering. Eventually, in 1063, it did surrender and announced its willingness to accept Duke William of Normandy as master of Maine. Norman historians of the time wrote that William made a joyous entrance into the city, with crowds cheering him. Robert was named Count of Maine, which was now part of Normandy. Count Walter of Mantes and his wife, who had been living in Le Mans, were turned over to William, who had them imprisoned. They died some time later, under mysterious and suspicious circumstances. It was believed by some that William may have had them poisoned.[2]

A Mysterious Journey

IN 1064, A SURPRISING EVENT OCCURRED THAT IS wrapped in mystery. For some reason, Harold Godwineson got on a ship in England and sailed across the English Channel. Where he was going and why he was going there are now completely unknown. Some accounts say he was sent by King Edward, to tell William he had been picked as Edward's heir. Another account says it was simply a fishing trip. At any rate, the ship was caught in a storm and wrecked off the coast of a region of France called Ponthieu, ruled by a count named Guy.

At that time, there were some barbaric customs for dealing with shipwrecked people. In some places, instead of helping them, they were often imprisoned and held for ransom! Guy had Harold and many of the people who were with him put in prison. However, Guy discovered who Harold was, and must have decided he could get more for Harold from Duke William of Normandy than by holding him for ransom. He notified William, who quickly

This scene from the Bayeux tapestry shows Harold on his way to see William.

arrived, apparently paid Guy a large sum of money, and took Harold to the capital of Normandy, Rouen.

William treated Harold very well. He gave lavish feasts for him, took him hunting, and even took him on a military campaign against the neighboring French province of Brittany. Count Conan, the ruler of Brittany, had shown himself to be an enemy, and William had been helping some people in Brittany who were in rebellion against Conan. Conan had pursued the rebels into a castle at a town called Dol, and was besieging them. They had managed to get a message to William, begging him for help. William could not ignore this of course, so he led a force toward Brittany and took Harold with him.

While the Norman army was crossing into Brittany, Harold performed an act of heroism that gained the admiration of all the Normans including William. The Normans were crossing a river near a towering fortified abbey called Mont-St.-Michel, with both men and horses wading through the water. The current was strong and some of the horses lost their footing and caused their riders to fall into the water. The men were in danger of being swept away and some were, but Harold managed to save several by plunging into the water and helping them make their way onto land. The Bayeux Tapestry shows him stepping out of the water with one man flung over his back and hauling another man out of the water by the arm.

Learning that the Norman army was approaching, Conan gave up the siege of Dol and retreated. William kept his army at Dol for a time, and then withdrew. No

THE BAYEUX TAPESTRY

A great deal of what is known about this event and the events that came after it, comes from a more than nine hundred-year-old, amazingly well-preserved medieval relic called the Bayeux Tapestry. The Bayeux Tapestry is a length of linen cloth, 230 feet long and twenty inches wide,

with scenes embroidered on it with colored wool thread. It is generally believed that the Bayeux Tapestry was created in the years between 1066 and 1082, by English craftsmen under the direction of Norman Bishop Odo of Bayeux, William's half-brother. It is currently on display, under glass, in a museum that was formerly the bishop's palace in the city of Bayeux.

The first scene shown on the tapestry is of King Edward talking with Harold, apparently ordering him to do something. The next scene shows Harold riding to the port of Bosham to board the ship that will take him across the Channel. He looks very much as if he is going on a hunting trip. There is a pack of hounds running in front of him, a hunting falcon perched on his wrist, and a group of knights riding behind. Further scenes show the ship caught in the storm, the capture of a bedraggled Harold by Count Guy, and the arrival of William.

sooner was he gone than Conan came back. Learning of this, William also returned. Again, Conan pulled back into Brittany and this time William followed, Harold with him.

Not too much is known about the war in Brittany, but it is known that the Norman army attacked a walled town called Dinant. The wall was made of wood, so William had his men attack it with flaming torches. The wall caught fire, the fire spread into the town, and the Breton defenders surrendered. This may have been the end of the campaign. Apparently, Harold took part in much of the fighting. By this time, he and William had become close friends.

HAROLD SWEARS AN OATH

Sometime either before or after the campaign in Brittany, William arranged for Harold to take an oath—make a solemn promise. To do this, Harold had to put his hands on chests holding bones of saints and make the promise aloud, before a group of Norman nobles and Church officials. The Bayeux Tapestry has a scene showing Harold doing this. It was an extremely sacred and religiously important action. People of the Middle Ages believed that anyone who broke an oath such as this, sworn on the bones of saints, would surely go to hell when they died.

The wording of the oath is not known. However, it is known that the oath required Harold to promise to do everything he could to see that William was chosen as king after King Edward's death. In later years, stories grew about the oath. It was said that Harold had not known there were saints' bones in the chests; this had been concealed from him. It is now known that this was not true, however. Another story was that Harold had been forced to swear the oath, perhaps being threatened with death if he did not. This might have been true, but it is not known for sure if it was.

William also got Harold to make other promises. At that time, throughout Europe, it was common for nobles to try to form alliances by arranging marriages between their sons and daughters. William got Harold to promise to marry one of his daughters, Adela, and to promise to send his sister to Normandy to marry a Norman noble. Harold agreed.

HAROLD RETURNS TO ENGLAND, PERHAPS WITH A PLAN

Late in the year 1064, Harold returned to England, bringing with him many gifts from William. Word of Harold's oath had been spread throughout Western Europe, and it seemed to most people that he had given up any claim he might have had to the throne of England. However, Harold may well have had other plans. He knew he was popular in England, much more popular than a Norman duke. He may have thought that if he could make people believe William had forced him to take the oath, or that William's claim to have been told he was Edward's successor was not true, they would be willing to accept him as king rather than William.

In the year that Harold returned to England, his brother, Tostig, had been Earl of Northumbria for about nine years. Tostig ruled with such harsh and unfair methods that he eventually brought on a rebellion. In autumn 1065, while Tostig was hunting in the south of England, the Northumbrian shires of Yorkshire and Northumberland exploded in revolt. A horde of Northumbrians broke into Tostig's palace in York, massacred his guards, and looted his treasury. They proclaimed Tostig an outlaw, and elected a young man named Morcar, the brother of the Earl of Mercia, to be their earl. They began to march southward, intending to have a meeting with the king and tell him of their demands. Men came swarming to join them from every town they passed through.

HAROLD ELIMINATES A RIVAL

Since Edwin Godwine's triumph over him in 1052, King Edward the Confessor had practically retired. He apparently spent most of his time following the progress of the huge church he was having built in the Westminster district of London. King Edward realized that Northumbria might well decide to break away from England and form an independent kingdom. He had come down with an illness, and was too ill to go and meet with the Northumbrians, so he had to pick someone to represent him. The logical person to do this was Harold Godwineson, of course. With his popularity and his skill at dealing with people, he could probably do the best job of calming the northerners down.

Harold agreed to be the king's representative. He rode out alone and met the Northumbrians in the city of Northampton. He listened to their demands, which were mainly that King Edward accept Morcar as the new Earl of Northumbria and that Tostig be banished from England.

This may have given Harold an opportunity he could not let slip by. Tostig was his main rival in England to become king, and if Tostig had to leave England, it would leave things clear for Harold. With what seemed to be great reluctance, he agreed to urge Edward to accept the Northumbrian demands.

When Tostig heard of this he apparently became furious and accused Harold of betraying him. He may have believed that Harold was just trying to get him out of the way in order to more easily become king. He had no choice, however, so he, his wife Edith, and their children went to live at the court of Count Baldwin of Flanders, who was Edith's half-brother.

EDWARD DIES AND HAROLD MAKES HIMSELF KING

Edward's illness grew worse. On January 5, 1066, he lay dying. The Bayeux Tapestry shows that there were four people with him. His wife, Queen Edith was crouched at his feet. Stigand, the Bishop of Westminster, was bent over him, giving him the last rites. His steward, Robert fitz Wimarc stood behind him, helping him sit up. Harold

Godwineson knelt at his left. Several of Edward's friends were invited into the chamber, but their names are not known and they are not shown on the tapestry. However, apparently one of them later made the statement that Edward had touched Harold's hand and in a faint voice asked him to take care of the queen and the royal household. This was certainly *not* a statement that Edward was naming Harold as his successor, but that was how Harold and his supporters took it. Harold called together a number of nobles who made an announcement that Harold Godwineson had been recognized as Edward's heir and would be the next king of England. Edward's funeral was held on the day after his death, and no sooner was it over than Harold rode to Westminster Abbey, and had himself crowned king.

So Harold could call himself king, but there were three men who all believed they had a better right to be king of England than he did, and were ready to use war or murder to take the crown away from him. These were his brother Tostig Godwineson in Flanders, a man named Harald Sigurdarson, the king of Norway, and William, the Duke of Normandy. Each of these men began to consider what they should do.

HAROLD RENOUNCES HIS OATH

Duke William apparently heard the news of Harold's crowning three days after it happened. He was outraged by Harold's breaking of his oath, of course. He sent a messenger to England to see Harold, reminding him that he had taken an oath on relics of saints. It was said that Harold told the messenger, "It is true that I took an oath to William; but I took it under constraint."[1] Harold meant that he had been forced to take the oath. This might have been true, for he was completely in William's power, and William could have threatened him with imprisonment or even death if he would not take the oath. If so, the oath would not have counted. However, to this day it is not known whether Harold took the oath willingly or was forced into it.

In his message, William also reminded Harold of the other promises he had broken: to marry William's daughter, and to send his sister to marry a Norman noble. Harold provided explanations for why he had not kept these promises, saying that it was against the will of the people of his country for him to take a foreign wife. As for the promise about his sister, he said, "she has died within the year, would he have me send her corpse?"[2] All the explanations may have been reasonable, but it certainly seemed that Harold was trying to make it look as if he had not done anything wrong in any way. William sent other messages to Harold, but the Englishman simply ignored them.

William realized that now, instead of merely going to England and being crowned as king, he would have to fight Harold and defeat him. This would mean a major war, beginning with an invasion and probably several battles. He would have to create a battle fleet and put together a powerful army. He also knew he had to try to cut Harold off from any possible help he might get, while gaining as much help for Normandy as he could.

An Unexpected Invasion

ONE OF THE FIRST THINGS WILLIAM HAD TO DO was call all his vassals together and let them know that he intended to wage a war of conquest against England. They were not all pleased about this, and in fact a number of them were very against it. Fighting to help William defend Normandy against invaders was one thing, but crossing the English Channel to fight a war against a country that did not seem to be of any danger to Normandy was another. Many of William's counts and viscounts let him know they thought this was more than should be asked of them.

According to a historian who wrote about this a number of years later, William's boyhood friend, William fitz Osbern, leaped to his feet and began to scold the men who were questioning their duke. "He is your master and requires your services," he told them. "It is your duty to come forward with a good heart and honour your obligations."[1] Before long, the opposition faded away, and

79

William's vassals promised to furnish William with ships and fighting men as needed.

WILLIAM GAINS STRONG SUPPORT

William next began sending messengers to the courts of Europe to see what help he could get from them. Henry IV, the ruler of the group of countries known as the Holy Roman Empire, promised aid. So did King Sweyn of Denmark. Counts and nobles of France and Flanders pledged their help. But the greatest source of help came from Pope Alexander II. William sent a group of Norman nobles to Rome to ask the pope to make a judgment on William's claim to the throne of England. They presented evidence that Edward the Confessor had named William as his successor, and provided information on the oath Harold Godwineson had sworn. It is not known if Harold was given a chance to send someone to present his side of the story, but he did not do so. This made it look as if Harold knew he could not prove that his claims were true. Accordingly, Pope Alexander publicly announced his support of William's claims and announced that he would have a holy banner made for William to ride under in battle. This made William's cause seem almost like a holy crusade, and men came flocking to Normandy from all over Europe to become part of it.

WILLIAM'S STRENGTH AS A LEADER

Many of these men were young knights with no land of their own and not much wealth. They all knew that if they helped William win a battle for the English throne, he would reward them with lands and high positions in England. Other men who came to join William were the kind of soldiers called mercenaries, who made their living by fighting for pay. But in addition to pay, a war in England would give them the chance to gain wealth by looting and robbing English farms and villages. Thus, the army building up for William in Normandy was a force of tough, hard, ambitious men, for whom warfare was a way of making a future for themselves.

Generally, a medieval army of that sort was very unruly and hard to keep under control. The men's usual way of getting the provisions they needed was to simply raid the surrounding countryside and take whatever was wanted. There might not be any killing but there certainly was robbery. However, William spread the word that raiding was absolutely forbidden. He saw that provisions were brought in from many distant areas, so the countryside where the army was encamped was never stripped bare as it might otherwise have been. This shows that William had firm control over his army, and that his commands were willingly obeyed. He was a strong leader.

BUILDING A FLEET, PROTECTING NORMANDY'S FUTURE

In spring 1066, William gave orders for ships to be built. The Bayeux Tapestry illustrates how this was done. Workmen with long-handled axes are shown chopping down slim trees and a carpenter with a long saw is pictured

A Norman ship from the time of William the Conqueror

splitting a log into planks. This leads into an illustration of shipbuilders fastening planks together to form hulls. The ships that the Norman shipbuilders created were very much like the dragon ships their Norse ancestors had made. They did not have grinning dragon heads on their fronts, but they were long and sleek, with a single mast at the center from which hung a big square sail. The tapestry shows that many of the ships were decorated with bright stripes of red, yellow, and black; or red, green, yellow, and black, running lengthwise from front to back. The sails, too, were striped, usually with stripes the same color as those on the hull, running from side to side or top to bottom.

At some time while the fleet was being built, William had to take care of some very important official matters. He was going to England to fight a battle, and there was always the chance that he could be killed. It was necessary for him to do what he could to make sure that the line of rulers descended from the first ruler, Count Rollo, would continue to rule Normandy even if William died in battle. Just as his father had named him heir, he now named his eldest son, Robert, who was fourteen years old, heir to become Duke of Normandy. He named his wife, Duchess Matilda, to be regent, ruling in William's name until

Robert became old enough to take over. In this way, William made sure that if he did not return to Normandy, the Norman nobles would not begin fighting among themselves to see who could become duke, as they had done when he was a boy.

TOSTIG AND THE KING OF NORWAY MAKE AN AGREEMENT

By about August 12, William's fleet, of perhaps some five hundred ships,[2] was ready. It assembled off the coast of Normandy and waited for the wind to become favorable for the voyage across the Channel.

THE OMEN IN THE SKY

In late April 1066, a certain event caused terror throughout Western Europe. There suddenly appeared in the night sky a fuzzy star with a long glowing tail streaming behind it. This was the comet now called Halley's Comet, which can be seen from earth about every seventy-seven to seventy-nine years. It was seen over Europe for seven straight nights, and caused great fear. The people of 1066 did not know what a comet was, of course, and they believed the glowing streak in the sky was an omen of terrible things that were going to happen. For the people of England, it was.

Tostig was also making preparations. He badly wanted to return to England and regain his power as an earl. He probably also wanted revenge on his brother Harold for forcing him to leave the country. Tostig knew that the King of Norway, Harald Sigurdarson, believed he had a good claim to be king of England. According to a tale written about Tostig many years later, he went to see King Harald and offered to help him conquer England.

Like many prominent people of that time, Harald had a nickname. He was known as Harald Hardrada, a Norse term that meant a stern and ruthless ruler. He was well over six feet tall, a striking height for a man of that time, and was a famous warrior. He had fought in his first battle at the age of fifteen. He believed he had a claim to the English throne because of something his nephew Magnus, who had been Norway's king before him, had done.

In 1040, the Dane named Harthacnut had ruled as king of both England and Denmark. Sometime between 1040 and 1042 Harthacnut apparently made a pact with Magnus, that whichever of them died first, the other would get his kingdom. When Harthacnut died in 1042, Magnus did get the kingdom of Denmark, but in England the Witan chose Edward the Confessor to be king. There was a story that Magnus sent a message to Edward telling him that he owned England as well as Denmark, because of his pact with Harthacnut. Another story was that Magnus considered invading England but was never able to put together an invasion force.

When Magnus died in 1047, his Uncle Harald became king. Now, Harald Hardrada announced that he had a rightful claim to the English throne because Magnus should have been the King of England as well as Denmark, and he, Harald, was Magnus's successor. He and Tostig agreed to work together to invade and conquer England.

TOSTIG STRIKES, HAROLD IS ALERTED

Tostig was first to act. In May, he attacked England with a small fleet of ships, manned for the most part by mercenary soldiers of Flanders. He raided the Isle of Wight, off the southern coast of England, for plunder and treasure. He was joined by one of his former Northumbrian followers named Copsi, who, like Tostig, had been banished from England and wanted to go back. Copsi brought seventeen ships, giving Tostig a force of about sixty. Together, Tostig and Copsi raided along the southern coast of England, in the earldom of Mercia. However, they were badly beaten by a force led by Earl Edwin of Mercia, and fled with only about a dozen ships left.

Tostig's raid may have made Harold realize that he had better put together a force to defend against the invasion that was known to be coming from Normandy. He raised a strong army of men from the southern shires along the southern coast where William was sure to try to land his invasion force. A fleet of ships was assembled and put in position off the Isle of Wight, which is directly across from Normandy in the English Channel. It is not known exactly how many ships Harold had, but it must have been at least one hundred.[3] The fleet's job was to watch for the coming of the Norman ships, attack them, and send word of their coming to the English army assembled on the coast. This was a good plan. William's ships would have to fight their way through the English fleet, and every Norman ship that was sunk or forced to turn back would mean fewer soldiers for William's army. Then, when what was left of William's ships would have reached the coast, his men would have had to try to fight their way ashore against men waiting on the beach for them—a terribly difficult thing to do.

TOSTIG AND HARDRADA INVADE

However, there were several drawbacks to Harold's plan. One was that with the English fleet collected in the south, there was nothing to stop an enemy fleet from landing troops much farther up the coast. The other was that the sailors on the ships and the soldiers guarding the coast would have to be fed and paid. The food would have to come from the farms of the shires along the coast, and providing enough food for the thousands of extra men in the area could become a problem over time. The longer it took for the invasion to happen, the more difficult things would become. Harold correctly expected that William probably intended to make his invasion some time in August, but he did not know that William's ships were lying at anchor on the Normandy coast waiting for the wind to change so they could sail. As the days of August dwindled into September, Harold began to worry about continuing to feed and pay his men. The food was beginning to run out in the southern shires, and so was the gold and silver in his treasury.

Meanwhile, in Norway, Hardrada put together a fleet of about three hundred ships[4] and sailed for England. In early September he was joined off the English coast by Tostig, with a few ships. Together, they had a force of about nine thousand men.[5]

On September 8, the provisions ran out for the English forces protecting the southern coast. Harold had to let the army disband, and ordered the fleet to come to London. On that same day, with nothing to stop them, the ships of Hardrada and Tostig sailed up the Ouse River into northern England. The Norwegian army disembarked about ten miles from the large important city of York, in Northumbria. The first invasion of England had begun.

WILLIAM STRIKES

MORCAR, THE EARL OF NORTHUMBRIA, AND Edwin, Earl of Mercia, quickly put together an army and marched to meet Harald and Tostig. A small portion of their army consisted of soldiers of the kind called *huscarls*, which meant "household warriors." They were well-trained soldiers of the kind who formed the small permanent armies of earls, nobles, and of the king. They wore coats of flexible mail, made of metal rings or small loops of chain linked together, and their heads were protected by cone-shaped metal helmets. They carried long shields that were rounded at the top and tapered to a point at the bottom, and were each armed with a sword and a long spear or a long-handled axe.

Most of these men rode horses, but they would dismount and fight on foot when the battle began. The English had no cavalry—men who fought on horseback— as the Normans did, nor did they have many archers. The rest of the army was formed mainly of what was called the *fyrd,* which were all the able-bodied men of a region who could be called together by the ruler to fight. These men were farmers and peasants and seldom had any thing such as armor or a helmet. Their weapons were generally just a spear, a pitchfork, or perhaps simply a club. Nevertheless, all these English soldiers had a reputation of being very fierce, courageous fighting men.

The Norwegians were armed and equipped very much like the huscarls, except that while not all of them had coats of mail, they almost all had helmets. Nearly all of them carried round shields made of wood reinforced with metal bands. Like the English, the Norwegians had no cavalry and very few archers.

A NORWEGIAN VICTORY

The two forces met on September 20, two miles from York, and a fierce battle was fought. Each side apparently was divided into two wings, with Harald and Tostig each commanding a wing of Norwegians, and Edwin and Morcar each leading a wing of English. The English and Norwegians fought very much alike, both sides mostly on foot, with close-up weapons such as swords, battle axes, and spears, but almost no bows. There was generally no battle plan on either side, men just rushed at each other and began hacking. Earl Morcar's Northumbrians formed the wing facing Tostig's force, and the Northumbrians showed they still held hatred for their former earl, launching a violent attack against him. However, the Norwegians promptly counterattacked, and the English line began to come apart. Soon, the English were running in all directions, with heavy losses. Many of them were chased into a swampy marsh behind them, where they were killed or drowned. It was said that the marsh became so filled with English bodies that the Norwegians were able to walk across it afterward without getting their feet wet. The battle, which became known as the Battle of Fulford, after a nearby village, was definitely a Norwegian victory.

Four days later, Harald arrived at York and ordered the city to surrender, which it promptly did. To make sure it held to the surrender terms he demanded hostages from among the wealthiest and most important people of Northumbria to be gathered at Stamford Bridge, eight miles from York. He then marched his victorious army back to where the Norwegian ships were anchored, to rest and celebrate.

HAROLD MARCHES FROM LONDON AND SURPRISES THE NORWEGIANS

The next day, Harald began marching the Norwegian force to Stamford Bridge. However, he made two rather serious mistakes. He did not think he would have to fight any more battles soon, so he left about a third of his army with the ships. He also had his soldiers leave their armor at the ships, so it would be easier for them to march without that extra weight.

In London, King Harold was astounded to hear of the Norwegian invasion in the north. He had not expected such a happening, but he knew he had to fight off the northern invasion before William struck in the south. He put together an army from London and the surrounding shires, and started it marching north at the fastest pace it could maintain. With him, and commanding portions of the army, were his brothers, Gyrth, Earl of East Anglia, and Leofwine, who had an earldom made up of the shires of Kent, Surrey, and several of those around London.

Harold's army, which was now the main army of England, was much like the English force that had been beaten in Northumbria. There was no cavalry and very few archers. A fairly large portion were huscarls, belonging to Gyrth, Harold, and Leofwine. The rest were fyrd-men that Harold ordered up out of the shires he passed through.

Harold's army was able to move quite fast because it was marching on roads that had been made by the Romans, who had once ruled England hundreds of years before. These were very well-made roads, straight and made of stone, which made marching easier. On September 25, the English army marched through York, headed for Stamford Bridge, and caught the Norwegians by surprise—without their armor and with a third of their force back with the ships anchored in the Ouse River.

TOSTIG REFUSES TO MAKE A DEAL

Very little is known today about the actual course of the battle that occurred at Stamford Bridge that day. There are some accounts of it that were written many years later, and may have come down from stories told by people who lived at the time, but many things in the accounts seem very unlikely.

One story claims that there was a parley, or peaceful meeting, between some of the leaders of each side before the battle began. On one side were Tostig and some of the Norwegian commanders; on the other were some of the English commanders. According to the story, one of the Englishman asked, "Is Earl Tostig in your army?"

Tostig stepped forward and told them who he was. The Englishman said, "Your brother Harold sends you greeting, and this offer. You can have peace, and all of Northumbria for your own. A third of the kingdom rather than no agreement." He was offering to make a deal. If Tostig and the men he commanded would stay out of the fight, Tostig could stay in England and be Earl of Northumbria again.

"It is a better choice than you gave me last winter," said Tostig, referring to when he was exiled from England, "but what does my ally King Harald of Norway get for his trouble?"

"Seven feet of English ground," the Englishman replied, "or, because he's taller than most, as much again if he needs it."[1] He meant that they would give Harald enough ground as was needed to bury him in. They were suggesting that Tostig betray Hardrada by staying out of the battle and letting him be killed.

"Go back and tell Harold to make ready for battle," Tostig told the Englishman, refusing to betray Harald Hardrada. The parley was over.

A FIERCE BATTLE WITH MANY CASUALTIES

Another story is that the Norwegians formed for battle on one side of the river, shoulder-to-shoulder with their shields all touching, making what was called a shield wall. To get to them, the English would have to cross a narrow bridge. However, there was a single Norwegian warrior standing at the end of the bridge, blocking the way. English huscarls charged forward to sweep him out of the way, but he cut down every one who reached him. Archers shot arrows at him, but he simply caught them on his shield. Finally, one of the huscarls noticed that there was a gap in the planks of the bridge where the Norwegian was standing. He waded through the stream beneath the bridge until he reached the gap, then he stabbed upward through the gap with his spear, killing the brave Norwegian. This is an exciting story, but most historians feel it is a bit far-fetched.

Other accounts indicate that the battle was long and hard. At about noontime, Harald Hardrada was hit in the throat by either an arrow or a spear, and died. Refusing an offer from his brother to discuss peace, Tostig took command of the Norwegian force and kept fighting. Some time in the afternoon he, too, was killed. A message had been sent to the Norwegian troops back with the ships, but they arrived too late and made no difference.

It seems fairly certain that the Norwegians took very heavy losses. Historians writing some years later stated that the loss of men was so bad that it was twenty-five years before Norway was even able to form another army. One man, writing some fifty or sixty years after the battle, stated that an enormous amount of bones still lay on the battlefield, indicating large numbers killed.[2] Another written account says that the Norwegians fled to their ships, and that while there were hundreds of ships anchored in the river, only about twenty-four sailed for home with men in them![3] Harald Hardrada did indeed get seven feet of English earth, but some years later his remains were dug up and delivered to Norway for burial there.

THE NORMAN FLEET SETS SAIL FOR ENGLAND

The battle, called the Battle of Stamford Bridge, was certainly a resounding victory for King Harold of England. However, both Stamford Bridge and Fulford were actually costly blows to the English army that was going to have to fight the invasion of the Duke of Normandy. The English had lost a lot of men, and the ranks of Harold's fighting force were seriously thinned.

All this time, Duke William's ships had sat off the coast of Normandy, waiting for the wind to turn favorable. On September 27 it finally did and William ordered the ships to be made ready for the trip across the Channel. The Bayeux Tapestry shows what took place. Pairs of men carried coats of mail, slung from poles, aboard ships. Others carried helmets, bundles of swords, spears, and axes. Wooden barrels and leather bottles of wine went onto

In order to invade the island kingdom of England, the Normans would have to build strong warships.

each ship, along with cooking pots, utensils, and dishes. Horses were led up ramps onto ships, about four horses to a ship. Everything was ready by nightfall, and the ships began moving out into the black water. William's ship, named the *Mora*, a gift from his wife, led the way. Matilda had spared no expense to make it a magnificent-looking vessel. At its prow, or front, was the carved head of a snarling lion, and at the back, but facing forward, was the gilded figure of a boy holding a trumpet to his lips. A burning lantern hung at its rear to guide the rest of the fleet.

WORRISOME JOURNEY, SAFE ARRIVAL

It was a moonless night, and the Channel was as black as an underground cave. In the middle of the Channel, the

Mora got separated from the rest of the fleet. There were no sounds of any other ships around it. No shouts from it into the darkness provided any answer. The Normans on the ship began to show signs of concern.

However, William showed no concern at all. He called for a meal to be served to him, and sat munching and drinking with obvious enjoyment, as calmly as if he were at home in his palace in Rouen. The other Normans regained their confidence. If William was not worried, why should they be? William was being a good leader, calming the fears of his followers. As the sky began to lighten, the other ships were sighted, some distance behind. All was well.

On the morning of September 28, the Norman ships began coming into a bay called Pevensey on the southern coast of England. William had probably expected to have to either fight his way through a fleet of English ships, or to find an English army lined up on the shore waiting to assault his troops as they tried to get onto land. Instead, he found an undefended coast, because Harold's provisions and money had run out some twenty days earlier, and he had been forced to disband the fleet and army that had been waiting to fight off the invasion. It was a tremendous piece of good fortune for William.

The ships were run up on the shore and the men began to disembark. They had been given instructions and nothing was left to chance. William and his commanders had planned for the possibility that they might have to fight their way ashore. First off were all the archers, with their bows strung and arrows in place ready to shoot. They spread out and moved forward, staring about for any sight of an English soldier.

Following the archers were the knights, in full armor and wearing their helmets. Their horses were led off the ships that had carried them and the knights quickly mounted. In groups they rode out into the countryside.

The next men to come off the ships were not soldiers. They carried hammers and shovels rather than weapons and their job was to prepare fortifications and defenses for the Norman army. On several of the ships they had brought with them sections of wooden walls that were cleverly contrived so they could be fitted together to make three fortresses. Working quickly and smoothly, the men put one of these together and dug a moat around it, making a small, crude castle that could be used as a place for storing supplies. The second invasion of England was under way.

The Battle That Won a Kingdom

WITH THE COMMON SOLDIERS ALL OFF THE ships, the commanders began coming ashore. According to one of the old stories about the invasion, as William stepped onto English soil he slipped, and fell forward, thrusting his hands out in front of him to break his fall.

At that time in history, a thing such as this, happening at the beginning of such an important event as an invasion, was considered an "*omen,*" or foretelling of bad luck. Men around William groaned, and some shouted, "an evil sign!" However, William raised his hands to show that each one held a clump of dirt that he had clutched as his hands had touched the ground. "See, my lords," he yelled in a cheerful voice, "by the splendor of God, I have taken possession of England with both my hands! It is now mine, and what is mine is yours!"[1] The groans turned to cheers.

If this actually happened, it shows that William was quick-witted enough to turn a negative event into a positive one. However, there are a number of very similar stories and legends from ancient and medieval times, and most historians think that this story was simply borrowed from one of them.

As the daylight began to fade into darkness, the Norman army settled down to its first day on English soil. An account of this event says that, "All then ate and drank enough and were right glad that they were ashore."[2] It had taken twelve hours for the whole army to disembark from the ships.

THE NORMANS LOOT AND RAVAGE THE COUNTRYSIDE

Pevensey was not a good place for an encampment because the land around it was marshy. The next day William moved his ships and men some ten miles eastward to where there was a bay and a town called Hastings. The other two wooden fortresses were put together and the Normans now had a base that would be easy to defend.

William knew that he could not simply sit and wait for Harold to appear. The supply of food in the surrounding countryside would be used up, and his men would have to go farther and farther to find more, which would put them at risk of attacks. He had to *make* a battle happen, soon. For that reason, he began to deliberately and cruelly harry the countryside. Soldiers were sent out to collect pigs, sheep, oxen, cheeses, sausages, flour, and even clothing from the farms and villages of the nearby countryside, but they also brutally destroyed the homes and fields of the farmers and peasants in the area. There is an illustration on the Bayeux Tapestry that shows a mother and her young child clutching each other's hand and running from their house as Norman soldiers set fire to it. By doing all this, William was forcing Harold to quickly come to the rescue of his people in the region.

Harold was in York, about five days after the battle against Hardrada, when a tired messenger came riding in from the south with word of William's landing, and of his destruction of the countryside around Hastings. Immediately Harold started his army marching southward. It reached London about October 6. Harold stayed there some five days to gather as many more fighting men as he could. Then he started marching south again, toward a region that was known in the Old English tongue as Santlache, meaning "Sand Lake." (Today, this region is called Senlac.)

THE ENGLISH FACE A DIFFERENT SORT OF ARMY

William had been sending groups of cavalrymen out every day, as scouts. Eventually, some of them caught sight of the approaching English force, and hurried to report to the duke. Harold knew he had been seen. He had hoped he could catch William by surprise but that was now impossible. On the evening of October 13 he put his army at the top of a grassy hill with a single ancient apple tree on its crest, about seven miles from Hastings, overlooking the region. He arranged his men in a close-packed block about six hundred yards long. The huscarls were in the front. Behind them were the fyrd men, with short throwing spears and throwing clubs. There were a few archers among them. Harold waited for William to come to him.

William's army had started out from its encampment before dawn, and as the sun rose it was spread out in the valley that stretched out at the foot of the hill. The two armies were about two hundred yards apart.

The army of Normandy was very different from the English army. About one-third of William's army of some seven to eight thousand men[3] were cavalry—knights on horses. The English, of course, had no cavalry at all. Another large portion of William's army was made up of archers. The English had almost no archers. The Norman archers did not wear armor and most wore leather caps rather than helmets. They carried bows that were four feet long and could send an arrow to a distance of two hundred yards. It could go through chain mail at fifty yards.

A SACRED BANNER AND A GIFT FROM THE POPE

William divided his army into three sections, and ranged them across the valley. On the left were the mercenary troops from the French provinces of Brittany, Anjou, and Maine, commanded by Count Alan of Brittany. On the right were men from all parts of France and Flanders, commanded by Count Eustace of Boulogne. In the center were the Normans, under William's half brother, Bishop Odo. One of the knights with them was William's boyhood friend, William fitz Osbern. At the front of each section were the archers, behind them the masses of foot soldiers, behind them the cavalry. William was with the Normans, under the banner that had been given him by the pope. There is no written description of what this banner looked like, but there is an illustration on the Bayeux Tapestry that may show it. Count Eustace of Boulogne is pictured riding behind William, carrying a banner. It is long and slim, with three pointed tails and with a red cross spread across a white background. With this banner whipping over his head, William ordered the army of Normandy to begin moving forward.

William was said to have also had another gift from the pope with him that day. Around his neck, beneath his armor, was a slim silver chain with a locket hanging from it. In the locket was a ring containing a hair said to be from the head of St. Peter, the first pope. It was believed that by wearing the locket with this holy relic in it, William would be protected from being injured or even killed.

A FIERCE AND BLOODY COMBAT

William began the battle some time after nine o'clock, by ordering his archers to fill the air with arrows aimed at the front line of Harold's men. The archers trudged forward to within some fifty paces of the English line and began shooting. In this way, William hoped to cut down Harold's numbers without risking any of his own men. Flights of arrows hissed toward the hill, but it was just a little too far and the archers were shooting uphill, so the English simply held their shields in front of themselves and took almost no casualties.

Soldiers on both sides fought fiercely during the Battle of Hastings.

The Norman archers pulled back and the foot soldiers moved forward. As they trotted toward the shield wall, they were met by a hail of spears, thrown clubs and axes, and a few arrows. They crashed into the shield wall and there was an instant din. Normans shouted their battle cry—"Deus aie,"[4] or "God aid us." They believed that because the pope had announced that William was in the right, God was on their side. The English replied with a great yell of "Out! Out!"[5] meaning that they intended to drive the Normans out of England. Swords clashed together. Swords and axes thudded into shields. There were screams of pain. The grass became spattered with blood.

Seeing that the English shield wall was holding, William ordered his cavalry forward. The horses plunged up the slope of the hill. The knights hurled their spears, drew their swords, and slammed into the shield wall. Their spears and swords and the impact of their horses gouged holes in the English line, but the horsemen found themselves facing the most terrible weapon of the English—the long-handled, two-handed battle axe. Viciously swung by sturdy English warriors, this weapon could cut through chain mail and take off a man's arm or leg, or cut through a horse's neck and take off its head! The Bayeux Tapestry clearly illustrates what a bloody fight this was, for it shows headless bodies, severed heads, and arms lying scattered beneath the hoofs of the Norman knights, horses and the feet of the English huscarls.

THE LEGEND OF TAILLEFER

There is a legend about the Battle of Hastings that tells how the Norman and French knights rode forward singing a song about a French hero named Roland, who had lived several hundred years earlier. According to the legend, a knight named Taillefer was with them. Taillefer was a minstrel, a musician who lived at William's court, and provided entertainment at feasts, by singing to the accompaniment of a harp. The legend tells that he called out to William, "A boon [favor], sire! I have long served you, and you owe me for all such service. To-day, so please you, you shall repay it. I ask as my guerdon [reward], and beseech [beg] you for it earnestly, that you will allow me to strike the first blow in the battle!"[6] William is said to have called back, "I grant it!" As Taillefer rode forward ahead of the others he twirled his sword and tossed it into the air as he sang. The legend says that as he reached the English shield wall, he struck a blow with his sword that killed an English huscarl. A moment later, he himself was killed by a blow from an English axe. While most historians think this is merely a made-up heroic tale, many feel it might be based upon something that actually happened during the battle.

WILLIAM TURNS THINGS
IN NORMANDY'S FAVOR

The battle began to go against the Normans. The section of the army formed from Brittany and the other French provinces began to come apart, with the knights galloping back down the hill, the foot soldiers running after them. The Normandy section's left side was left uncovered and unprotected, and the whole section began to fall back.

This was the moment when Harold might have won the battle if he had done the right thing. If he had ordered the whole shield wall forward it could have wiped out all the Norman archers and foot soldiers in its path. Only the knights on their horses could have gotten away.

But no order to advance was given, and now something happened that turned things back in the Normans favor. William, with the Norman section in the center of the army, was knocked off his horse in the commotion that was taking place. A shout went up that he had been killed. He quickly remounted his horse and shoved his helmet up on his head so that his face could plainly be seen. Then he went galloping along the front of the entire army, shouting as he went, "Look at me! I am alive, and by God's help, I shall win!"[7]

With cheers, the Normans stopped pulling back and with William leading them began to move forward. The section of French troops, on their right, moved with them. On the left, the troops from Brittany got themselves back in order and began to move forward with the others.

William led his soldiers to a decisive victory at the Battle of Hastings.

For several hours, the Norman army continued to assault the English shield wall with no result. Finally, William decided to try to use a trick. He spread the word, and at a signal, the whole army turned around and began to move off as if it were giving up.

A cheer went up from the English, and they began to yell insults after the apparently retreating Normans. Several thousand of them broke out of the shield wall, and began to run after the Normans, hoping to be able to kill or wound some of those at the rear.

This was probably exactly what William had hoped. He had kept his knights at the front of the attacks on the shield wall, so now they were at the rear. Trumpets sounded, and the knights promptly wheeled their horses and went charging into the Englishmen who had been coming at them from behind.

The English had no chance. They were all on foot and spread out in an unorganized mob, with no shield wall around them. They were slaughtered by the many hundreds.

Harold's army had taken serious losses. William now ordered his archers to pour arrows into the English, but now he instructed them to shoot high, so the arrows came down on the English from above. To save themselves, they had to raise their shields over their heads—but this left their bodies exposed to the spears of the Norman knights and foot soldiers. The shield wall's losses began to increase.

Harold's Death Ends the Battle

It was at about this time, with the sun near setting after almost a whole day's fighting, that Harold was killed. According to stories of the battle, he looked up, probably to see the position of the sun, and a Norman arrow came slicing down out of the sky and tore into the corner of his eye. He pulled it out and actually tried to keep fighting. Suffering from loss of blood as well as the sight of one eye, he was unable to defend himself and was hacked to death by the swords of several Norman knights, one of whom, it was said, may even have been William.

There is some doubt about how Harold was killed. While the Bayeux Tapestry does show an armored English soldier with an arrow in his eye, he seems to be just an ordinary huscarl. Next to him is another armored Englishman lying on the ground and being trampled by the horse of a Norman knight, and many historians have thought this was actually Harold. However he was killed, Harold was dead, and both his two brothers had been killed as well, so the English army had no leaders. It began to come apart as men turned and fled. It was said that William sat on his horse clutching the stump of his spear, which had been broken in the fighting, and watched his enemies run. The Battle of Hastings, which is sometimes called The Battle of Senlac, was over. The number of casualties on each side, dead and wounded, is unknown.

ENGLAND FIGHTS THE CONQUEST

IN MEDIEVAL TIMES, IT WAS CUSTOMARY FOR soldiers of armies that had won a battle to loot, or rob the bodies of dead soldiers of the army that had lost. This was actually regarded as a form of payment for common soldiers. Generally, the bodies of the dead men were completely stripped. All clothing was taken because it could either be used or sold, and there was often jewelry or money hidden in it. Thus, the battlefield of Hastings was littered with naked dead bodies, many of them horribly disfigured by wounds.

Shortly, William had many of these bodies carried away from the center of the battlefield to create a large clear area. There, a large tent, which had been brought on one of the Norman ships, was set up, to which the chief Norman commanders all came. A huge feast was prepared by William's famous cook, a man named Wadard. Surrounded by the dead bodies of their foes, the Norman conquerors sat down to celebrate their victory.

This map shows William's and Harold's marches before the Battle of Hastings in 1066. By 1087, William had conquered much of England and had gotten Scotland, Wales, and Maine to pledge allegiance to him.

On the day after the battle, the mother of Harold Godwineson sent word to Duke William that she would give him the weight of Harold's body in gold, if he would give the body to her so she could bury him. William was perfectly willing to give her the body, but it could not be found. No one could tell which one of the many naked corpses was Harold. Eventually, someone was located who could identify Harold by a mark, perhaps a mole, on a particular part of his body. His body was identified, and William had him buried on the battlefield where he had fought. Many years later, the body was moved to the town of Waltham, where Harold had built a church in 1060.

WILLIAM BEGINS A MARCH ON LONDON

Following the battle, William had gone to the camp at Hastings and began to wait for the earls, bishops, mayors, and rulers of shires to come and offer him obedience, as was customary. But he was not immediately accepted as king by the English people. Many of them were calling for the throne to be given to a fourteen-year-old boy known as Prince Edgar, who was a great grandson of Ethelred, who had been king of England fifty years earlier. Being related to a former king gave Edgar a better claim to the throne than William had.

After five days passed, William decided that he had better throw a scare into the English, to let them know they were conquered. He started his army marching toward London. When some soldiers of his army foraging for food were killed by citizens of a town called Romney, William responded savagely. Houses were burned and people were hanged. The lesson sank in. The big important port city of Dover sent word of its surrender, followed by the city of Canterbury.

Then, something that could have changed the course of history occurred. A serious epidemic of dysentery broke out in the army. Dysentery is a horrible disease that causes torturing stomach pain and severe loss of body fluid. It can cause death, and there was no treatment for it nine hundred years ago. Norman and French soldiers became ill by the many hundreds, and even William was stricken. If the English had been able to put together an army and make an attack, they could have probably wiped out William's army and made him a prisoner. But they had no leaders. In time, although the Norman army suffered serious losses from the disease, it was once again on the march toward London.

LONDON SURRENDERS, WILLIAM IS CROWNED KING

There was no sign from London that it intended to surrender to William. William did not intend to attack London if it did not give in to him; he chose to simply cut it off from the rest of England. When his troops reached the outskirts of the city, he had them gradually surround it, and burn some of the outermost sections. Finally, the Archbishop of Canterbury, the English earls Edwin and Morcar, Prince Edgar himself, and other high officials of the city came out and acknowledged William as their new ruler.

William knew that he was resented and hated as the conqueror of England, and knew he might well face an uprising some day. He had to be able to hold London if this ever happened. He had his soldiers begin the construction of several castles inside the city. One of these was built in the east side of the city, on the north bank of the Thames River, which runs through London. This became William's home and the place where he made all his plans. At first it was just a wooden structure on a mound of earth within a wooden wall with a ditch around it, like the castles of Normandy in William's boyhood. As years went by it became covered with stone, and as centuries went by it became a cluster of buildings. Today, it is the place known as the Tower of London, which is a major tourist attraction of England.

On the morning of Christmas Day, 1066, William was crowned king of England. It was a noisy and frightening event, because some of William's soldiers became alarmed by the milling crowds and thought a rebellion was taking place. To control it, they set fire to some buildings near the cathedral. Smoke started to creep into the cathedral and a reddish glow seeped through the windows. People began leaving, to try to help fight the fire. It was said that even William himself appeared to be rather nervous. However, the ceremony continued until the crown was finally placed on his head. He was now King of England and Duke of Normandy.

WILLIAM PUTS DOWN A REVOLT

William soon began making changes. Many of the English officials were allowed to keep their positions, but others were replaced by Normans who had fought with William at Hastings. William broke Harold Godwineson's big

A coronation ceremony signfied the start of William the Conqueror's reign as king of England.

earldom of Wessex into small pieces and gave them to his special favorites. His half brother Odo was named Earl of Kent, and his best friend, William fitz Osbern, was made Earl of Hereford.

William was now accepted throughout Europe as the legal king of England. But there were still a great many English people who certainly did not accept him. England was not truly conquered. Many English people still thought of Prince Edgar as the rightful king of England.

For a time things remained quiet, and in March 1067 William returned to Normandy. He was King of England but he was also still Duke of Normandy, and had to look after things there. He took with him a great many English nobles and officials, among them Prince Edgar, the earls Morcar and Edwin, and the Bishop Stigand. They were treated as honored guests, but actually these were all people who, if left behind in England, might have become leaders of a revolt. William was trying to prevent this.

Nevertheless, late in the year, a revolt did flare up in the city of Exeter, in southwest England. William hurried back, crossing the Channel on December 6. He quickly put together an army that included English soldiers willing to fight even their own people for pay, and marched to Exeter in bitter winter weather. Exeter was well fortified and its people refused to open the gates. William began a siege, making attempts to break through the walls. This went on for eighteen days, and William's force took heavy losses. However, the people of Exeter could see it was only a matter of time before William's troops broke into the city. When that happened, they knew they would be killed by the many hundreds, and the city would probably be burned down. They sent word to William offering to surrender. William let them off easily, but he had a castle built in the city and filled it with Norman troops that could act instantly and harshly if another revolt should break out.

SHOWING OFF THE KING

By spring 1068 things were quiet enough so that William felt safe in bringing Matilda over from Normandy. On Whitsunday, the seventh Sunday after Easter, she was crowned queen of England in a splendid ceremony.

Splendid ceremonies of that sort were really quite important. The symbols of a king were a crown and a scepter, which was an ornamental rod. Even some nine hundred years ago, kings did not walk about every day wearing a crown and carrying a scepter. Generally, William probably just looked like a well-dressed man. However, there were times when William, quite literally, had to play the role of a king, and then he put the crown on his head, held the scepter in his hand, and probably had an ermine-trimmed robe draped around his shoulders. This was done at meetings of the Great Council, which were held at Christmas, Easter, and Whitsuntide, the week beginning with Whitsunday. On these occasions, the king had to be shown in all his glory, to all the people who could be squeezed into the great hall of one of the castles of a major city such as Gloucester or Winchester. There, with candlelight gleaming off his golden crown, he represented the royal might of England. That it was an impressive sight is proven by the fact that on one occasion, a man in the hall was reported to have shouted out, "Behold I see God!"[1] This was probably the way most people at that time thought God must look, like a king with a robe and crown.

REBELLION IN THE NORTH

No matter how splendid William and Matilda might look, many English people were still not at all happy with a Norman king and queen. Prince Edgar had managed to slip away to Scotland with his mother and sister, and was under the protection of the Scottish King, Malcolm. His supporters in England were stirring up opposition to William, and in the summer of 1068 there was a flare-up of rebellion in the north. William dealt with it by marching north and building castles in the cities of Warwick, Nottingham, and York. Into every castle went a force of Norman soldiers. The building of all these castles was a move of military strategy by William. A castle was not merely a fortress for defending a place; it was actually also a weapon of *offense*. It could be used as a base for a force of knights that could quickly ride out and attack anywhere in the countryside. Even a small force of Norman mounted knights could generally overcome a much larger force of foot soldiers.

After a time, William felt free to take a trip to see how things were in Normandy. He was still in Normandy in early 1069, when an English rebel force attacked York. The people of York promptly opened the city to them and declared loyalty to Prince Edgar. William came rushing back from Normandy, gathered up a fighting force, and took it on a hurried march to York. He moved so quickly that he caught the rebel force by surprise, outside the city, and almost wiped them out. He built another castle in the city and put more Norman soldiers in it. William may now have felt that things were not safe enough for Queen Matilda to remain in England, for she soon returned to Normandy.

A DANISH FORCE INVADES ENGLAND

Perhaps because of all this unrest and disorder in England, Sweyn, the King of the Danes, now decided to move against William. Danes had ruled England for twenty-six years, and apparently still felt they had a claim on the country. In August of 1069, despite the fact that he had pledged aid to William in 1066, King Sweyn sent a powerful fleet to the east coast of England. It was 240 ships strong,[2] commanded by his sons Harold and Cnut, and his brother, Osbern. The Danes landed a strong force near York and were joined by rebel forces led by Prince Edgar. In September the Danes and their rebel allies stormed York. The city was nearly destroyed by fire that was apparently set by the Norman forces trying to defend it. One of the Norman castles was captured but the other managed to hold out and send a message to William. The Danes took the treasure and plunder they had looted from York and went aboard their ships anchored in the Humber River. Their rebel allies marched away.

In January 1070, William came north with a strong army. Now he began to use incredibly harsh and cruel measures to show his power and bring the rebellion in Northumbria to an end. Crops were piled together and burned, livestock animals were slaughtered, people were driven out of their homes and the homes burned. Nothing was left to such people—no home, no food, no hope. An English writer who lived through all this wrote that more than one hundred thousand men, women, and children died of starvation as a result of William's harrying of the land. Corpses lay rotting along the roadsides, corpses of starving people who had grown too weak to continue walking in search of food, and had simply lain down to die. The writer said of William, "He cut down many in his vengeance; destroyed the lairs of others, harried the land and burned homes to ashes."[3] The land was so thoroughly devastated that seventeen years later it was still barren and uninhabited.

THE CONQUEST COMPLETED

IN MAY 1070, KING SWEYN OF DENMARK CAME to join his fleet. It sailed south, into what was called the fen country. This was a region of low marshy land, much of which was under shallow water most of the time. In the heart of the fen country was a tiny island called Ely. There was a force of English rebels on Ely, led by an English noble by the name of Hereward. He was known as Hereward the Wake, a word that meant someone who watches. The rebels had fortified Ely with a wall of turf and a fence of heavy logs, and made it their base of operations against King William. It was an excellent base, well protected, impossible to get to except by boat, and with abundant food available—fish, eels, and waterbirds such as ducks and herons. Sweyn put a force of Danes ashore on Ely to join forces with Hereward and his rebels.

To this day there are many legends about Hereward, some of which may be true. It was told that as a boy he had saved a child from a savage bear by killing the animal with a single thrust of a sword. He was said to have served as a soldier in wars in Flanders, Cornwall, and Ireland as a young man. He returned home some time after William's conquest of England and found that his brother had been executed for killing two Normans who were trying to take over the family's lands. This made Hereward decide to fight against William and the Normans.

GETTING RID OF THE DANES

A tiny town and a monastery, the Abbey of Peterborough, stood on dry ground not far from Ely. One of William's supporters, a Norman named Turold, had taken over the abbey with a force of soldiers. He was using it as a base from which to dominate and terrorize the English people of the region. In June, the Danes and Hereward's rebels on Ely made a surprise attack on the abbey. They sailed from Ely in boats, probably at night, and landed at a point not far from the abbey. Moving quietly they reached the abbey, where no watch was being kept, and easily broke in. Catching Turold and his men completely by surprise, they wiped them out. They then burned the abbey to the ground, so it could not be used as a Norman base again. When word of this came to William he knew he had a serious problem on his hands. He put together an army and marched into the fen country.

William's main need was to somehow get rid of the horde of Danes menacing Northumbria. He preferred not to have to do battle with them, because if he lost, all of England might explode in revolt against him and he could lose his kingdom. But there was another way. He managed to get Sweyn to meet with him at some time in the summer, and during the meeting William apparently offered the Danish king an enormous bribe to simply sail away back to Denmark. Sweyn accepted, and in the summer of 1071, the Danes departed.

HEREWARD'S REBELLION IS BROUGHT TO AN END

Without King Sweyn's help, Hereward's rebellion was doomed, but he and his followers continued to hold on in Ely, defying William's efforts to either wipe them out or make them captives. They were joined by many Englishmen who were willing to fight William, among them the Earl of Northumbria, Morcar. This long period during which William was trying to find a way to capture Ely and Hereward's men were holding it against him, gave rise to many more legends about Hereward the Wake.

One of the most exciting of the Hereward legends tells of a time when he disguised himself as a ragged peddler and actually went into William's camp to try to find out what William's plan of attack on Ely would be. What he supposedly found out was that William was having a large and sturdy bridge built across the marshes to the edge of Ely. However, before Hereward could get out of the camp with this valuable information, he became involved in a brawl with a Norman soldier and was made a prisoner and bound with chains. According to the legend, Hereward bided his time until he was able to free himself from the chains. Then he used them to knock his guard unconscious and escape.

It is not known whether William actually had a huge bridge built, as the Hereward legend states, or not. Another story claims that William assembled a huge fleet of boats and invaded the island with them. Still a third story is that a group of monks on Ely showed William a secret route to the island. Whatever happened, the island was finally captured and the rebels surrendered. William was apparently very lenient with them. Hereward vanished and what became of him is not known.

WILLIAM BRINGS SCOTLAND TO ITS KNEES

Beyond Northumbria lay the Kingdom of Scotland, where King Malcolm ruled. There were no exact borders then, and no one was quite sure where England ended and Scotland began. Malcolm apparently began to fear that all of William's activity in Northumberland and the English north country showed his intention to gobble up Scottish land. He began to raid into the area between Scotland and Northumbria, as if attempting to make it useless to William.

In 1072, William decided he had to go into Scotland with land and sea forces and settle the situation. In the autumn he entered Scotland with an army made up mostly of Norman and French knights and a large fleet moving off the coast nearby. Malcolm constantly pulled back, avoiding getting into a battle, and finally agreed to meet with William at the town of Abernathy. The result of this was that Malcolm swore a pact with William, officially acknowledging him as king of England, and pledging peace. He had been letting Prince Edgar stay in Scotland, but now he agreed to send him away, so he could not lead any more rebellions.

Edgar's departure from Scotland was the last thing needed. There was now no one trying to become king in

This silver penny is from the reign of William the conqueror and bears his image.

William's place. There were no threats from the countries on England's borders. There was peace throughout England. The conquest was complete.

TROUBLE IN BOTH NORMANDY AND ENGLAND

Early in 1073 William was back in Normandy with a large force of troops he had brought from England. He had a problem to take care of. In 1072, while William was busy in England, some of the people of the province of Maine had invited the Count of Anjou to take charge. This would mean Maine was lost to Normandy. William intended to prevent that. He invaded Maine. The Count of Anjou and his troops left the province. By the end of March 1073, Maine was once again firmly in Normandy's hands.

This move of William's made several enemies. The Count of Anjou, Fulk le Rechin, was of course angered. Count Robert of Flanders was angered. The King of France, Philip I, was angered. Philip was probably irritated that a man who was actually supposed to be his vassal was now a king, equal to him, and that Normandy was generally regarded throughout Europe as more powerful than France.

Meanwhile, trouble was again brewing in England. Many of the nobles from the French province of Brittany, who had accompanied William to England and fought at Hastings, had been given land and titles in England and were living there. A number of these men had died since 1066, and their lands and titles had been inherited by sons.

THE NEW FOREST

William was passionately fond of hunting, and, of course, the best place to hunt was a forest. He discovered an area of land of about one hundred square miles, in the shire of Hampshire that was an untouched forest. He decided to turn it into a royal preserve, a forest in which only he and his guests could hunt. However, it seemed just a bit too small. There was an area of open land adjoining it, of about thirty square miles, on which some five hundred families lived, about two thousand people.[1] William ordered them all to leave and had their houses burned to the ground. The deserted land that remained

Hunters like William often looked for deer in English forests.

was added to the preserve and trees were planted on it. The entire region became known as the New Forest.

William apparently gave no thought to what would become of the people he had chased out of their homes. It did not seem to matter to him that they had lost everything they had. However, in this way, he was really no different from most of the kings and nobles of his time, who gave little thought to any problems of the common people. The New Forest became his private hunting place and he decreed laws to protect the animals that lived in it. Any commoner who was discovered to have killed a New Forest deer to feed his family was punished by being blinded—having his eyes put out.

In 1075, for some reason, many of these young men decided to revolt against William. It is hard to understand why they wanted to do this, for they were all wealthy and powerful because of William's generous grant to their families. Their ringleader, Ralf of Gael, was Earl of Norfolk and owned land in both Brittany and England. Another rebel was Earl of Hereford, and still another, Earl of Huntingdon. Perhaps they simply wanted more wealth and power. At any rate, they hatched a plan, began raising armies, and sent messages to Denmark offering deals in return for help. The Danes always seemed willing to try an invasion of England, and Cnut, the Danish king, put together a fleet of two hundred ships and prepared to sail to England.[2]

THE REBELLION DEFEATED, A PERSONAL TRAGEDY

William the Conqueror had left the English government in the hands of Archbishop Lanfranc, a Norman that William had made Archbishop of Canterbury in place of the English Archbishop Stigand. When the revolt began, Lanfranc wrote to William urging him to stay in Normandy and assuring him that his loyal followers in England could handle things.

They did. An army formed by Norman lords and religious leaders met the little rebel force led by Ralf of Gael and forced it into retreat. Ralf fled England to his land in Brittany and settled down in a castle at the town of Dol. Another little rebel army led by Earl Roger of

Hereford was smashed by a Norman-English army, and Roger was captured and imprisoned for life. The Earl of Huntingdon was eventually executed by having his head chopped off. When the fleet of Danish ships arrived, the revolt was over. The Danes made some raids on York and places on the coast, and left.

While all this was going on, William was also troubled by a personal tragedy. His second son, Richard, was killed in a hunting accident in the New Forest. It is not known how old he was, but he was probably quite young, perhaps only a teenager. Many English people regarded the young prince's death in the forest William had made as punishment of God on William, for his cruelty in driving so many people out of their homes in order to make the forest bigger.

SETBACKS, TRIUMPHS, AND A SON IN REBELLION

In September 1076, William brought an army into Brittany and put the castle of Dol, where Ralf de Gael was living, under siege, intending to teach Ralf a lesson. However, in October, King Philip of France brought a large army to Dol to Ralf's aid. Apparently there was a battle, although nothing is known about it, and William was beaten and forced to leave Brittany.

This was a serious blow to William's reputation, and it encouraged some of his other enemies to make further attacks on him. Late in 1076 or the early months of 1077, Fulk le Rechin, Count of Anjou, attacked the castle of one of William's chief supporters in Maine, John of Le Flech. John was able to hold out until William could come to his aid, and Fulk withdrew. This was a setback to the people opposed to William, and eventually a truce was declared between William and Fulk and Philip I.

This did not prevent further attempts to discomfort William. Between Normandy's eastern boundary and a river called the Oise was a region known as the Vexin. It was a divided region, with half belonging to Normandy and half to France. When the count of the Vexin decided to become a monk and entered a monastery, leaving Vexin without a ruler, Philip marched an army in and seized control of all the Vexin. This was certainly an insulting challenge to William.

There was nothing William could do about the insult, because something far more serious and troubling to him had occurred. His eldest son, Count Robert of Maine, was now about twenty-five years old. He was quite popular and had a great many friends among the younger members of William's court, but he was inclined to be overconfident and do things without thinking them over first. He had always been on the best of terms with his father, but now, suddenly, he demanded that he be given control of both Maine and Normandy. William, of course, refused Robert, for this could have caused a tremendous uproar in Normandy. Robert stormed out of the court and with a number of his friends actually tried to seize control of the city of Rouen, the capital and heart of Normandy.

William had to act at once. He ordered the immediate arrest of everyone involved. This could have meant imprisonment and even death for many. Robert and most of his friends fled Normandy.

Robert began to seek help for his plan to take over Normandy. He visited his father's enemies, King Philip and the Count of Flanders, and began to gather followers from throughout France, Brittany, Maine, and Anjou. They gathered together at a castle King Philip furnished them. It was obviously the beginning of a full-fledged revolt.

A Last
Campaign

WILLIAM BROUGHT AN ARMY AGAINST THE
rebel's castle and put it to siege. The unexpected
happened. The rebels surged out of the castle, fought a
pitched battle against William's force, and William's troops
were defeated. William himself was knocked off his
horse—possibly by his own son—and wounded. He and
his troops fled. It was the worst humiliation William had
in his life.[1]

William returned to Rouen and sent word to his son
asking for a meeting. Robert came with some of his
supporters, and talks began. They lasted almost a year, but
by the end of 1079 William and his son were together
again. William pledged that when he died, Robert would
become Duke of Normandy.

When news of William's problems reached England
and Scotland, Malcolm, the Scottish king, knew he could
do as he wished and William would not be able to stop
him. He led an army into the upper part of Northumbria,

where he raided and plundered from mid-August to the second week of September. When no army came from William to punish this action, many people of Northumbria grew angry. Some of William's officials were murdered, and in May 1080, the royal castle at Durham was attacked.

With the situation in Normandy as bad as it was at this time, William was not able to get back to England until late July 1080. He put his brother Odo in command of an expedition to punish the rebels in Northumbria, and sent his son Robert in command of a force to punish Malcolm in Scotland. Robert forced Malcolm to renew the agreement he had made with William in 1072.

ANOTHER INVASION THREAT

Once again, with William out of Normandy, his enemies there tried to gain advantages. Fulk, the Count of Anjou, marched into Maine, heading toward Normandy. William hurried to cross the Channel with a large force of Norman and English troops, and advanced into Maine. It was said that a huge battle was on the verge of being fought but was somehow prevented by a number of monks and priests, but there is no actual record of this, only stories. However, something caused Fulk and William to come together and sign an agreement similar to the one they had signed in 1077.

For a time, things ran smoothly. But then, in 1082, William and his brother Odo had a quarrel. The reason for the quarrel is uncertain, but William went to England and had Odo seized and brought to Normandy, where he was imprisoned.

Some time near the end of July 1083, there was another quarrel, this one between William and Robert. Once again Robert left Normandy, and became the center of opposition to William throughout France. In November, Queen Matilda died, but even her death did not bring William and Robert together again.

By 1085 William had become hugely fat and his health was failing. Everyone knew that King Cnut of Denmark was planning another invasion of England with the help of King Philip of France and William's son, Robert. William began preparing. He had stretches of the English coast laid waste, so that the Danes would be unable to find food when they landed. He brought a larger number of fighting men into England than had ever come into the country before.

THE DOMESDAY BOOK

At Christmas time that year, William came to the English city of Gloucester. There he held long, serious discussions with his council about matters in England. He had a great plan to tell them about, a plan for finding out the value of everything owned by the English people—land, animals, and money.

During the next year, 1086, most of England was divided up into districts, generally formed of two or three shires. Hundreds of men began going through England on William's orders, visiting every district. In each district, a priest and six common people were put under oath to answer all questions asked them by William's men. Thus, in each district a record was made of every person who owned land and the amount of land and other property they owned. A written account of this survey, made at that time, says that not one yard of land, not one ox, cow, or pig was overlooked.

When the survey was completed, it was bound into two books, which became known as Domesday Book. The exact meaning of this title is not known. The word dome, or doom, was the Old English word for a judgment, or a law, written down by a king, and Domesday is the term for the Day of Judgment that is predicted in the Christian Bible. Does the title Domesday Book refer to the biblical day of judgment, or does it simply mean a day when Englishmen were judged for their wealth or value? No one is certain. However, nothing like this book was ever produced by any other country in Western Europe during the Middle Ages. It is the only such thing of its kind.

A GREAT OATH IS SWORN

William's main reason for doing this was that he needed money and needed to know where he could get it. The enormous number of mercenary soldiers he had brought to England to fight against the Danish invasion when it came had to be paid. To pay them, he had to collect taxes and raise money. Accounts in the Anglo-Saxon Chronicle and other places say that William's methods of doing this were savage and brutal. The Anglo-Saxon Chronicle said that

William "did not care how sinfully the reeves [king's money collectors] had got it from poor men, nor how many unlawful things they did."[2]

As 1086 began, Cnut (also spelled *Canute*) of Denmark built up the war fleet and army with which he planned to invade England. However, there was widespread resentment among his people about this. In July, as Cnut entered a church in the Danish town of Odensee, he was assassinated. This ended the danger of invasion, but the situation for William was still perilous. Robert was still in revolt, Odo was writing treasonous letters from prison, and Philip I was still scheming.

In August 1086, William held a great court in the city of Salisbury in southern England. The Anglo-Saxon Chronicle says that he ordered every landowner in England named in the Domesday Book to come there and swear allegiance to him, only. In other words, even a man who was someone's vassal now had to swear to obey William the Conqueror before the man whose vassal he was What William accomplished with this was to change feudalism in England and make himself the most powerful king in Europe! No earl or other noble could ever raise a rebellion against him, because their vassals could not fight against him if he ordered them not to. They would not dare break their oath of allegiance.

WILLIAM'S LAST CAMPAIGN

Some time in late 1086 or early 1087, William returned to Normandy. King Philip of France still regarded him as an enemy, and may have been responsible for events that brought trouble in the late summer of 1087. A small force of French soldiers came across the border of Normandy from the town of Mantes, in the French region of Vexin, and began to rob the peasants. In addition to this, it seems that William learned that Philip had been making jokes about him because he was so fat. It was said that William became enraged and swore to have revenge. In early

This seal of William the Conqueror shows him on horseback, carrying a flag and shield.

137

August he crossed the Vexin border with an army and headed for Mantes. On the way there he mercilessly harried the countryside he passed through, butchering peasants and burning houses. On the outskirts of Mantes, French soldiers tried to make a stand, but the Norman knights massacred them. The Normans entered the town and William allowed them to run wild. They killed most of the men, set the whole town ablaze, and burned it to the ground.

The destruction of Mantes was William's last act as a military commander. It is not known exactly what happened, but as William rode through the burning town, he either was suddenly stricken by some severe intestinal illness or was thrown from his horse and injured internally. In terrible pain he was carried back into Normandy, to Rouen, by his soldiers.

THE LAST DAYS OF A KING

William lay in the monastery of St. Gervais near Rouen for six weeks, in constant pain, obviously dying. During that time, despite his pain, he took care of his affairs. Two of his sons spent time with him, as well as his half-brother Robert and a number of Norman church and government officials, and he discussed matters with them. His son Robert, who was living at the court of King Philip, never came to see him; they had become enemies. However, William made it clear he had promised Robert that he would be Duke of Normandy upon William's death, and he did not intend to break his promise. He made the statement that he forgave Robert for becoming a rebel against him.

William had named his second son after himself, but because of his son's red hair and reddish complexion he was known as William Rufus, or William the Red. King William told William Rufus he wanted him to be the next

WILLIAM'S SONS AS KINGS

William Rufus became King of England after his father's death, but he turned out to be a very bad king, disliked by almost everyone. He was denounced by the clergy of the Church in England for his brutality toward the people and his attempts to take away the Church's rights. He was killed by an arrow while hunting in the New Forest and while this was officially described as an accident; many people believed it was actually an assassination. The English clergy refused to give him a church funeral. As had happened at the death of his younger brother, Richard, in the New Forest, many English people believed that William Rufus's death in the New Forest was punishment from God against Duke William's family, for William's cruelty in turning hundreds of people out of their homes to make the New Forest bigger.

Henry, William's youngest son, was crowned King of England after William Rufus's death, and turned out to be a pretty good king. He worked to bring together the English and Norman people of England, and took steps to keep the barons from gaining too much power over the common people.

king of England. However, William had not become a king through a family relationship as most kings did, but by bloody conquest. He did not know if the people of England would accept his son as their king. William told William Rufus to go to England, act as if he were the rightful king, and see what happened. William left for England at once.

That left only William's youngest son, Henry, to be looked after. Henry is said to have asked William, "And what do you give me, my father?" William replied that he was leaving Henry five thousand pounds of silver from his treasury. This was a sizeable sum of money, but Henry pointed out that it might not do him much good if he had no piece of land to call his own. Henry might have felt that he would not be welcome in Normandy when Robert took it over, and perhaps William Rufus would not have welcomed him in England, either. He apparently left his father's bedside without another word.

It is not known if any of William the Conqueror's daughters came to see their father as he was dying, or if he made any attempt to provide for them. Two were in religious orders and the others were married. Perhaps he felt they were all provided for.

Death and Humiliations

WILLIAM SAW THAT WRITTEN INSTRUCTIONS were provided for a number of other things he wished to do. He ordered that a large amount of silver be distributed among the poor. He ordered that the churches in Mantes that had been destroyed when he had the town burned down, be rebuilt. He ordered that everyone who was presently in prison on his orders be set free, except for one person—his half brother, Bishop Odo of Bayeux. Whatever had caused William to become enraged with anger at Odo, he still had not gotten over it.

His other half brother, Robert, and all the Norman nobles urged him to relent about this, however. He finally gave in to their pleas and ordered Odo released. Apparently, Odo did his best to try to get to Rouen before his brother died.

It was said that sometime before he died, William made a deathbed speech in which he spoke about the things he had done. This may or may not be true, but a copy of what is supposed to be the speech was written by an Englishman who became a monk in Normandy some years after William's death. According to this man, William began by saying, "When my father decided to go on a pilgrimage and committed the duchy of Normandy to me I was still a young boy, only eight years old; from that day to this I have always borne the burden of arms."[1] What he meant by this was that since he was eight years old, he had always been involved in some way with warfare and battles. "I was brought up in arms from childhood, and am deeply stained with all the blood I have shed," he declared.[2]

THE DEATH OF WILLIAM

On the morning of September 9, 1087, the sound of a church bell ringing roused William out of the deep sleep or coma he was in. He asked why the bell was ringing. One of the people with him answered that it was the bell of the church of St. Mary, ringing the hour of Prime, the second of the seven hours the Church divided a day into. Hearing this, William muttered a short prayer, and apparently immediately upon finishing it, died. He was fifty-nine or sixty years old.

No sooner was William dead than the remains of this man, who had been hailed as a mighty conqueror and who had changed history, began to suffer humiliation and disrespect. The bishops and nobles rode off and his body was left alone. Neither soldiers nor anyone else were left to guard it. Servants, peasants, and others converged on the room and thoroughly looted it. They took furniture, pillows, and bed coverings, and everything of any use or value that could be carried off. William's body was left lying half-naked on the floor.

William had requested to be buried in the Monastery of St. Stephen, which he had built, in the town of Caen. His funeral turned into a humiliating and horrifying event. First, as the funeral procession was entering Caen, it was forced to stop and wait because part of the town was on fire! A large number of mourners had gathered to attend the funeral, but most of them left to help fight the blaze. William's body was left with only a few monks to accompanying it to the abbey.

A HORRIFYING BURIAL

As the funeral sermon was drawing to a close, a second humiliation took place. A man by the name of Ascelin, a citizen of Caen, suddenly got to his feet and began to speak. He announced that the land the abbey stood on had belonged to his father and now belonged to him, and that William had taken it by force. He shouted out that he refused to allow the body of a thief to be buried on his land—unless he received fair payment for what was owed him. A number of Ascelin's neighbors joined him to announce that what he said was true, the land was rightfully his.

For Normans, legal rights were enormously important. Thus, with William's body still unburied, the funeral was halted once again while a deal was worked out. Ascelin accepted a small sum of money from William's son Henry,

WILLIAM'S DISRESPECTFUL TREATMENT AFTER DEATH

The humiliations William's remains suffered after his death did not end with his burial. Nearly five hundred years later, during the late 1500's, there were flare-ups of religious civil war between Roman Catholics and Protestant Huguenots in France. In 1562, Huguenots completely ravaged William's tomb, which was heavily decorated with Catholic symbols. Most of his skeleton was scattered and lost, with only one of his thighbones remaining. It was preserved, and later, when Catholics regained control of France, it was buried under a new, ornately decorated monument.

However, during the French Revolution, at the end of the 1700's, many monuments to French nobles were destroyed by peasants. They wanted to wipe out all memory of France as a land ruled by kings, dukes, and counts. In 1793, William's monument was demolished, and some historians believed that the thighbone in it was either thrown away or destroyed. Today, a plain stone slab with only William's name and title engraved on it lies in the cathedral of St. Stephen, in Caen. It is generally believed that William's thighbone, the last bit of him left, lies beneath it.[3] But perhaps not. There may be nothing at all left of the man who became known as William the Conqueror.

along with a pledge from him and all the bishops present at the funeral that the full amount of the value of the land would be paid. Ascelin agreed and the funeral resumed. The body was carried to the coffin, in front of the altar.

However, the final humiliation, and the horror, now took place. The coffin provided for William was made of stone, and it turned out to be much too small. When an attempt was made to force his huge body into it, the decomposing body burst open, and a horrible stench flowed through the church. Priests hurriedly burned incense in an attempt to overcome the smell, but the service had to be cut short.

WILLIAM AS DUKE AND KING

As Duke of Normandy, William actually had to spend most of his time fighting to hold on to his position. Then, once his position was secure, he spent a great deal of time fighting to make Normandy a larger and more powerful province. Thus, most of his time in Normandy was spent in planning and organizing campaigns, and in marching to, and fighting in, battles. Because of his firmness, Normandy was actually the strongest and most peaceful region in all Western Europe at the time of his death.

What sort of a king was William? At the time he became king, a poet who lived then said of him, "Cold heart and bloody hand now rule the English land!"[4] He was not well-liked by the English people. A portion of the Anglo-Saxon Chronicles written by an English monk in the year William died discusses both his good and bad sides. It says that he was "a very wise man, and very powerful and more worshipful and stronger than any predecessor of his had been."[5] However, it also says "he was a very stern and violent man, so that no one dared do anything contrary to his will. He had earls in fetters [chains], who acted against his will."[6] As both a soldier and a ruler he was capable of great cruelty and harshness, but was really no worse than any other powerful person of his time.

William is regarded as a great general and a good leader of men. His great victory, The Battle of Hastings, was what historians call a "decisive battle," meaning a battle that truly changed history. It was not an instant change, like what happened when America won the Revolutionary War, and a new nation was created. Instead, it set the stage for gradual changes. We cannot guess how different things might have been from the way they are now if William had not won, but his victory brought about changes that might never have occurred, and that helped make the world the way it is today. For one thing, without William's conquest, the English language would be very different. For another, England, known today as a land of castles, would have far fewer castles, and some of the most famous ones would not even exist.

A DIVIDED NATION

The first result of William's victory was that it completely changed the people who ruled the Kingdom of England— the king and his counselors, the earls, the archbishops, and bishops. These had been men who were born and reared in

England, but within only a few years they were all replaced by men who had been born and reared in Normandy and other parts of France—Frenchmen. The Normans and other Frenchmen who helped William conquer England became the rulers of England, but they were very different from the previous rulers. Their ways of thinking about things and doing things were very different.

Thus, for several generations after William's crowning as King of England, there were two groups of people living together in England, but having as little to do with each other as possible. One group was the Normans. They were the earls, barons, bishops, and archbishops who now ran England's government and churches—those who had come from Normandy and other parts of France, and those who had been born among them since. They spoke mainly French, with a bit of Anglo-Saxon when necessary. All official records and legal documents of the kingdom were written entirely in French or Latin.

The other group was the Anglo-Saxons. They spoke only Old English among themselves and a bit of French when they had to speak to Normans. Even though the two groups lived side by side in the same country, and most of them had been born there, there was no unity among them. For generations, they still thought of themselves as either Normans or Saxons.

ENGLAND BECOMES PART OF WESTERN EUROPE

But gradually this changed. In order to talk to their rulers and to understand government and legal records,

Anglo-Saxons had to learn some French. Thousands of French words became part of the Old English language, and at the same time, the pronunciation of many Old English words changed. Eventually, a new language existed that was spoken throughout England by everyone—the language known as Middle English, the beginning of what we now call English. A new people had also been created, who now all called themselves Englishmen.

Having Frenchmen as England's rulers brought about a very important change. It took England out of the influence of the Norse countries. For hundreds of years, England had been affected mainly by what happened in Denmark, Norway, and, to some extent, Sweden. These were countries that had emerged out of an uncivilized, barbaric past. Now, with England ruled by Frenchmen, it came under the influence of France and Western Europe, which had risen out of the rich, civilized culture of the Roman Empire.

As time went on, England became more and more involved with the politics and culture of Western Europe. Instead of remaining a more or less second-rate kingdom, occasionally scuffled over by Norse kings, it came to be regarded as a significant member of the western European nations. Eventually, it created a great empire that played a major role in the world for hundreds of years. Many historians believe that this might not have happened if William and his Normans had not conquered England and changed it in the ways they did, by breaking its ties to Scandinavia and making it part of Europe.

CHRONOLOGY

1027 or 1028—William is born to Duke Robert and a commoner girl named Arlette or Herleve.

1035—Duke Robert leaves on a religious pilgrimage after getting his nobles to accept William as his heir.

1035—*July:* Duke Robert dies in Asia Minor. William becomes Duke William II of Normandy.

1040—Three of William's guardians are assassinated. Feuds and quarrels break out among Norman nobles. An attempt is made on William's life.

1046—A group of Norman nobles led by Guy of Burgundy revolt against William. King Henry I of France brings an army into Normandy to help William.

1047—*January:* William and King Henry defeat the Normandy rebels in the Battle of Val-ès-Dunes.

1051—Earl Godwine of Wessex and his sons rebel against King Edward of England and are exiled from England. About this time William is apparently notified that he is the successor to the throne of England.

1051 or 1052—William and Matilda, daughter of the Count of Flanders, marry.

1052—*Summer:* Count William of Arques rebels against his nephew, Duke William.

1053—*November or December:* Duke William captures Arques.

1054—*February:* French forces invade Normandy; Norman forces route the French at the Battle of Mortemer.

1057—*August:* Duke William overwhelms a French army at the Battle of Varaville.

1063—Duke William invades and conquers the province of Maine.

1066—*January 5:* King Edward the Confessor of England dies.
January 6: Harold Godwineson is crowned King of England by his supporters.
September: Northern England is invaded by King Harald Hardrada of Norway and Tostig.
September 20: An English army is overwhelmed by the Norwegian force.
September 25: The Norwegians are destroyed by an English army under King Harold at the Battle of Stamford Bridge,
September 28: Duke William's Norman army lands at Pevensey, on the southern coast of England. The next day William moves his forces to the town of Hastings.
October 14: William defeats the English army at the Battle of Hastings. Harold is killed.
December 25: William is crowned King of England in London.

1067—*March:* William returns to Normandy.

1069—*January:* The city of York is besieged by rebel forces, led by the English prince, Edgar.
August: A Danish fleet brings support to the rebels attacking York.
September: York is occupied by rebels. William recaptures it by Christmas.

1070—William makes a brutal march of destruction through the north to crush the rebellion, burning crops and homes and killing thousands.

1071—*Summer:* The Danish fleet leaves. Rebels hold the island of Ely.
October: William attacks Ely and the rebels surrender.

1072—*Autumn:* William invades Scotland, forces the Scottish king to sign a pact.

1073—William invades and reconquers Maine.

1075—A group of earls revolt in England. They are defeated by William's supporters.

1076—William attacks earls' stronghold in Brittany and is badly defeated.

1078—William's eldest son Robert revolts against his father in Normandy.

1082—William has his brother, Odo, imprisoned in Normandy.

1083—William's son Robert again revolts against his father.
1085—*December:* William holds court in Gloucester, presents his plan for Domesday Book.

1086—*August:* William administers "The Salisbury Oath" in Salisbury. William returns to Normandy.

1087—*Summer:* William invades the French Vexin, sacks and burns the town of Mantes. He is either injured or becomes ill.
September 9: Very early in the morning, William dies.

CHAPTER NOTES

CHAPTER 1. A CONQUEROR IS BORN

1. Gwyn Jones, *A History of the Vikings* Revised Edition (Oxford: Oxford University Press, 1984), pp. 219–220.

2. National Geographic Staff, *The Age of Chivalry* (The National Geographic Society: 1969), p. 68.

3. G. G. Coulton, *Medieval Panorama* (New York: Meridian Books, 1964), p. 58.

4. Allan Lloyd, *The Making of the King, 1066* (New York: Holt, Rinehart and Winston, 1966), p. 65.

5. National Geographic Staff, *The Age of Chivalry* (The National Geographic Society, 1969), p. 101, per William of Malmsbury.

CHAPTER 2. GROWING UP IN DANGER

1. Allan Lloyd, *The Making of the King, 1066* (New York: Holt, Rinehart and Winston, 1966), p. 61.

2. Eric Linklater, *The Conquest of England* (Garden City, N.Y.: Doubleday & Company, Inc., 1966), p.172.

CHAPTER 4. A BATTLE AND A SIEGE

1. David C. Douglas, *William the Conqueror, The Norman Impact Upon England* (Los Angeles: University of California Press, 1964), p. 50.

2. R. Allen Brown, *The Normans and the Norman Conquest* (New York: Thomas Y. Crowell Company, Inc., 1968), p. 59.

3. Allan Lloyd, *The Making of the King, 1066* (New York: Holt, Rinehart and Winston, 1966), p. 72.

4. Ibid., p. 75.

5. Douglas, p. 370.

6. Ibid.

7. Ibid.

CHAPTER 5. FIRST CONQUEST

1. R. Allen Brown, *The Normans* (New York: St. Martin's Press, 1984), p. 33.

2. Ibid., p. 37.

CHAPTER 7. VICTORIES AND MYSTERIES

1. David C. Douglas, *William the Conqueror, The Norman Impact Upon England* (Los Angeles, University of California Press, 1964), p. 172.

2. Ibid., p. 410.

CHAPTER 8. A MYSTERIOUS JOURNEY

1. E. S. Creasy, *Fifteen Decisive Battles of the World: From Marathon to Waterloo* (New York: Da Capo Press, 1994), p. 177.

2. Ibid.

CHAPTER 9. AN UNEXPECTED INVASION

1. Allan Lloyd, *The Making of the King, 1066* (New York: Holt, Rinehart and Winston, 1966), p. 159.

2. Ibid., p. 166.

3. Ibid., p. 179.

4. David C. Douglas, *William the Conqueror, The Norman Impact Upon England* (Los Angeles: University of California Press, 1964), p. 193.

5. Gwyn Jones, *A History of the Vikings*, Revised Edition (Oxford: Oxford University Press, 1984), p. 410.

Chapter 10. William Strikes

1. Eric Linklater, *The Conquest of England* (Garden City, N.Y.: Doubleday & Company, Inc., 1966), p. 201.

2. Major General J.F.C. Fuller, *A Military History of the Western World, From the Earliest Times to the Battle of Lepanto* (New York: Funk & Wagnalls Company, Inc., 1954), p. 370.

3. Matthew Bennett, *Campaigns of the Norman Conquest* (Oxford: Osprey Publishing Limited, 2001), p. 36.

Chapter 11. The Battle That Won a Kingdom

1. E. S. Creasy, *Fifteen Decisive Battles of the World: From Marathon to Waterloo* (New York: Da Capo Press, 1994), p. 182.

2. Ibid.

3. Major General J.F.C. Fuller, *A Military History of the Western World, From the Earliest Times to the Battle of Lepanto* (New York, Funk & Wagnalls Company, Inc., 1954), p. 372.

4. R. Allen Brown, *The Normans* (New York: St. Martin's Press, 1984), p. 20.

5. R. Allen Brown, *The Normans and the Norman Conquest* (New York: Thomas Y. Crowell Company, Inc., 1968), p. 169.

6. Creasy, p. 192.

7. Matthew Bennett, *Campaigns of the Norman Conquest* (Oxford: Osprey Publishing Limited, 2001) p. 46.

Chapter 12. England Fights the Conquest

1. David C. Douglas, *William the Conqueror, The Norman Impact Upon England* (Los Angeles: University of California Press, 1964), p. 258.

2. Allan Lloyd, *The Making of the King, 1066* (New York: Holt, Rinehart and Winston, 1966), p. 224.

3. Matthew Bennett, *Campaigns of the Norman Conquest* (Oxford: Osprey Publishing Limited, 2001) p. 56, per Orderic Vitalis.

CHAPTER 13. THE CONQUEST COMPLETED

1. David C. Douglas, *William the Conqueror, The Norman Impact Upon England* (Los Angeles: University of California Press, 1964), p. 371.

2. Ibid., p. 232.

CHAPTER 14. A LAST CAMPAIGN

1. Eric Linklater, *The Conquest of England* (Garden City, N.Y.: Doubleday & Company, Inc., 1966), p. 256.

2. Matthew Bennett, *Campaigns of the Norman Conquest* (Oxford: Osprey Publishing Limited, 2001), p. 87.

CHAPTER 15. DEATH AND HUMILIATIONS

1. R. Allen Brown, *The Normans* (New York: St. Martin's Press, 1984), p. 44.

2. Ibid., p. 45.

3. David C. Douglas, *William the Conqueror, The Norman Impact Upon England* (Los Angeles: University of California Press, 1964), p. 363.

4. Allan Lloyd, *The Making of the King, 1066* (New York: Holt, Rinehart and Winston, 1966), pp. 227–228.

5. Matthew Bennett, *Campaigns of the Norman Conquest* (Oxford: Osprey Publishing Limited, 2001), p. 87.

6. Ibid., p. 88.

Glossary

abbey—A dwelling place for monks or nuns.

abhorred—Hated.

accoutrements—A soldier's equipment.

allegiance—Loyalty to a leader or region.

culture—The art, literature, customs, and way of life of a nation or particular region.

decomposing—Rotting.

denounced—Spoke against.

ermine—The white winter fur of a species of weasel.

exiled—Forced to leave one's country or homeland.

hawking—A form of hunting, using a trained hawk to capture a bird or small animal.

medieval—The Middle Ages, from about 500 A.D. to 1500 A.D.

monastery—A dwelling place for monks.

parley—A discussion with an enemy before a battle.

pasteurized—Highly heated to destroy bacteria.

penance—A punishment accepted to show sorrow for doing wrong.

predecessor—A person or thing that came before another.

regent—A person specially selected to rule when the actual ruler is unable to, due to absence, disability, etc.

successor—A person expected to be given a position of rank or importance presently held by another.

FURTHER READING

BOOKS

Crompton, Samuel Willard. *Hastings*. Philadelphia: Chelsea House Publishers, 2002.

Davis, Ken. *The Kings & Queens of England*. New York: HarperCollins, 2002.

Hilliam, Paul. *William the Conqueror: First Norman King of England*. New York: Rosen Publishing Group, 2005.

Leaders of the Middle Ages. New York: Rosen Central, 2005.

Tilton, Rafael. *Rulers of the Middle Ages*. Detroit: Lucent Books, 2005.

INTERNET ADDRESSES

The Battle of Hastings
<http://www.battle1066.com/intro.shtml>

Invasion of England, 1066
<http://www.eyewitnesstohistory.com/bayeux.htm>
Click on "Middle Ages/Renaissance." Select "Invasion of England, 1066."

William I, William the Conqueror (c. 1028–1087)
<http://www.bbc.co.uk/>

INDEX